AboraMana
Wisdom

Script

Neithard Horn

4880 Lower Valley Road · Atglen, Pennsylvania 19310

The names Lilt / Lilth and Ygdrasil / Yggdrasil are used interchangeably in this text intentionally as used by the Goddess and author. Other varied name spellings and interesting combinations may also be included in the Wisdom according to channeled guidance.

All text and artwork by Neithard Horn
Copyright © 2011 by Neithard Horn
Library of Congress Control Number: 2010940733

All rights reserved. No part of this work may be reproduced or used in any form or by any means—graphic, electronic, or mechanical, including photocopying or information storage and retrieval systems—without written permission from the publisher.

The scanning, uploading and distribution of this book or any part thereof via the Internet or via any other means without the permission of the publisher is illegal and punishable by law. Please purchase only authorized editions and do not participate in or encourage the electronic piracy of copyrighted materials.

"Schiffer," "Schiffer Publishing Ltd. & Design," and the "Design of pen and ink well" are registered trademarks of Schiffer Publishing Ltd.

Type set in Book Antiqua/Garamond
ISBN: 978-0-7643-3696-6
Printed in China

Schiffer Books are available at special discounts for bulk purchases for sales promotions or premiums. Special editions, including personalized covers, corporate imprints, and excerpts can be created in large quantities for special needs. For more information contact the publisher:

Published by Schiffer Publishing Ltd.
4880 Lower Valley Road
Atglen, PA 19310
Phone: (610) 593-1777; Fax: (610) 593-2002
E-mail: Info@schifferbooks.com

For the largest selection of fine reference books on this and related subjects, please visit our website at www.schifferbooks.com
We are always looking for people to write books on new and related subjects. If you have an idea for a book please contact us at the above address.

This book may be purchased from the publisher.
Include $5.00 for shipping.
Please try your bookstore first.
You may write for a free catalog.

In Europe, Schiffer books are distributed by
Bushwood Books
6 Marksbury Ave.
Kew Gardens
Surrey TW9 4JF England
Phone: 44 (0) 20 8392-8585; Fax: 44 (0) 20 8392-9876
E-mail: info@bushwoodbooks.co.uk
Website: www.bushwoodbooks.co.uk

Dedication

The Myth of AboraMana
Goddess of Life, Love, and Beauty
is dedicated to all women on planet Earth

— Contents —

Foreword
Page 6

—

Getting Acquainted With Your Deck
The Five Suits of the Deck
Page 6

—

Introduction
Biographical Notes
Author's Note
Page 8 - 14

—

Declaration of Spiritual War
Page 15

—

The Ray of Creation
The Basic Layout Using All Cards of the Deck
Page 16

—

Description and Explanation of the Cards
Page 17 to Page 171

—

00 – The All-Including Truth
Page 17

—

The Jokers
Page 19

—

The Hall of God
Page 29

—

The Science of Physics
Page 43

—

Magic Physics
Page 52

—

The Science of Biology
Page 69

—

Magic Biology
Page 81

—

Human Kind
Page 95

—

The Temple
Page 108

—

You
Page 141

—

Laying Out and Reading the Cards
Page 172

—

Aloha and Mahalo
Postscript
Page 175

—

About the Author
Page 176

Foreword

This work you have in your hands consists of a deck of 89 cards and this script which explains the cards and the system of the deck. The art work for the cards was channeled by the Living Goddess, starting in May 2004 in a cave above the Puerto de Tazacorte on La Palma, Islas Canarias. Since October 2005, the painting of new cards continued on Kaua'i Island. At the same time, I received text to the cards and wrote it down.

The deck is expressively made for women as a massive counter weight against the male-dominated society of today with the historical and spiritual background of a male-dominated religion with a caste of male priests who preach subtle but merciless the devaluation of humankind in general and the devaluation of woman in the very particular.

The deck is neither a new version of Tarot, nor is it a deck of the genre of oracle cards. It is an illustrated cosmology, presented in the form of a religion, that explains the human position in the grand scheme of creation for the first time from an exclusively woman's point of view in a logical, holistic, and scientifically correct manner.

However, the deck can be used for divining and reading. Then it can help a woman to change how she understands herself, and how she can change her position in the society she finds herself in. This script and the deck is a handbook, a book to work with, a new tool. So don't expect "easy reading." The longer you work with it, the more it will open and the whole idea will make more and more sense to you.

The open intent of this work is to start you to rethink everything you thought until now by showing you one possible alternative line of thinking. What you've seen as Black, you're now supposed to see as White—that's it in a nut-shell.

Getting Acquainted With Your Deck

Find yourself a long table or kitchen counter out of the wind and lay out the whole deck in the order found under the title "The Ray of Creation" on page 16 of your script.

In the upper left corner of the frames of the cards you'll see little squares with numbers inside. They are color codes that designate the Plane of Creation and the number of the plane this card belongs to. Same colors and same numbers belong together in one plane. The first card "00 – Zero" and the last card "Eternity" both have no color code or number.

In the top center of the frame is the title of the Group this card belongs to. All cards of one group lay horizontally next to each other. With a new title, a new group begins.

The lower part of the frame shows the running number and the title of the card. The higher the number, the further down along the Ray of Creation the card has its place.

You'll find that some cards have the same number but different titles. Those two cards belong together; they complement and enhance each other.

In your script, in the beginning of each new Plane you'll find the order of the groups I found most logical and therefore most pleasing.

When gathering the cards to put them back in the box you can put them in order from the last to the first card, or just put them back as they come. Only take care that the Zero-Card is the uppermost card when you close the lid.

In case you want to gamble...

The Five Suits of the Deck

The House of Air

Y1 – Gryffa – Recklessness
07 – Space
11 – Gate of Air
15 – Empress of Air
19 – Air – Visual Arts
30 – Deva of Orchid
31 – Deva of Colibri
51 – Grace for the Flowers
54 – Our LovelyOne
59 – Dancer of Air – Lyrics
71 – The Naked Truth
72 – The Veil of Maya

The House of Fire

Y2 – Kentoura – Flexibility
09 – Energy
12 – Gate of Fire
16 – Empress of Fire
20 – Fire – Poetry
32 – Devi of Papaya
33 – Deva of Rooster
50 – Cleanse with Fire
55 – The Bitch
60 – Dancer of Fire – Drama
73 – Feathers
74 – Roots

The House of Water

Y3 – Minataura – Perseverance
08 – Matter
13 – Gate of Water
17 – Empress of Water
21 – Water – Music
34 – Devi of Coral
35 – Deva of Cowry
49 – Cleanse with Water
57 – LilithYggdrasil
61 – Dancer of Water – Rhythm
75 – TreeDweller
76 – CaveDweller

The House of Stone

Y4 – Sphinga – Patience
10 – Time
14 – Gate of Stone
18 – Empress of Stone
22 – Stone – Sculpture
36 – Devi of Oak
37 – Deva of Lizard
52 – Thanx for our Food
58 – The Ancestors
62 – Dancer of Stone – Style
77 – Day
78 – Night

The House of AboraMana

25 – AboraMana
26 – Life
27 – Death
28 – Queen of Devi
29 – King of Deva
42 – True Love
43 – The Gate of AboraMana
46 – Lilith AboraMana
53 – Prayers Answered
56 – The Mother
63 – Dancer for AboraMana
79 – Eternity

Introduction

AboraMana is the total sum of biological life on planet Earth imagined, perceived, and interacted with as a Goddess with a distinct personality and history. She is that mysterious energy we call Life, and we see every individual living being, be it bacteria, lichen, plant, bird, fish, animal, including human, as one of Her many children, and each one is one cell of AboraMana's body.

ABORA (stressed on the first *A*) is the name of the Energy of Life in the language of the extinct indigenous people (the Arehuca) on the Island San Miguel de La Palma, Islas Canarias. All thirteen tribes lived in matriarchy, women dominated the society, family chains were matrilineal and they perceived the Energy of Life as a female power called Abora—as it was documented by the first Spanish monks who came with the conquistadores.

Just for one or example: Every woman was born noble, every man was born as a commoner. Every man could apply to the tribe elders to be elevated to be a nobleman, which meant not only status but also clearly defined privileges and obligations. During his trial in front of the whole tribe he had to answer certain questions, and one of the questions was: "Did you ever treat a woman without respect?" And now imagine: All the women and girls of the tribe watching him and listening to his answer.

MANA is the name of the Energy of Life in the language of the Hawai'ians. They lived and live in a patriarchy, therefore Mana is perceived as a male power.

The name *AboraMana* suggests the balance of the female and male power in the biological creation, but we see the female power as the source of everything that is born, lives, procreates, and dies. She is a woman because all biological life comes into life through the woman, the mother.

AboraMana's official title is Goddess of Life, Love, and Beauty.

As the Horned Goddess, She is the Goddess of Fertility and Abundance. The horns stand for the cow as the symbol of tranquility and motherhood.

In the dark nights, She becomes the Goddess of the Black Moon, Her horns showing the crescent of the waxing and waning moon. She stands for the emotional wisdom and the intuitive decisions of the woman; the snake is Her symbol. The snake also stands for the feminine sexuality.

In Her form as a serpent She is the Chaos Goddess, the Goddess of Disorder, the moment the primordial soup exploded into Life with infinite possibilities open.

She is also the Fountain of the Power of Love because, according to our legends, God the Creator of the Universe of Physics, the cool engineer, the endless cosmic driving force, became the unconditional all-loving Father through Her love.

She is also called Our Mother Without Navel, because She Herself has no mother.

She is honored in four appearances, one in each of the Four Elemental Houses: Air, Fire, Water, and Stone. As the Goddess in the Elemental House of Water she is called:

Lilith AboraMana
Goddess of Life, Love, and Beauty
Goddess of Fertility and Abundance
Fountain of the Power of Love
Our Mother Without Navel

The rose is the sign of Her suit in the deck.
The rose is beauty, red is love, and the green leaves are life.

Since this work—deck and script—focus on a SupremeBeing, on God and Goddess, and the Host of Heaven and human's relation to the PowersGreaterThanUs; and since the goal of the work is to make this society a better society by spiritual and artistic means, it is a religious work; it was given to me to pass it on to you in the form of a religion, without my intention.

Please don't hold me responsible for what is revealed in the deck. My Goddess gave the visions of the cards to me; She revealed the system of the deck to me, She writes the text for me; it is *Her* work. I do nothing except listen to Her and do what She tells me to do.

And just like you, I'm asking: *Why did She choose me—a male—to speak up for Her and womankind?*

Working as an independent male in this male-dominated society makes life easier and the work has more chances to achieve the intended impact. (I realize that things are changing to the better, but are still a far cry from what it should and could be.)

Living as a male in this male-dominated society is a richer life because a male has more possibilities of experience. Just imagine traveling to remote places. A woman still can't do it safely, and here I'm not thinking of war-zones.

This work is filled with erotic and sex as the highest expression of Biological Life. Erotic and sex work best between opposite sexes—no matter what humans with homosexual preferences claim—because we were created with opposite sexes, and we live in a dual world. I love my Goddess so much more because I am a man and She is a woman. And She knows it, and She reveals Herself ever more to me like a loving woman undressing for her man.

The Spiritual Universe of AboraMana

Goddess, Life
The Creator of the Universe of Biology

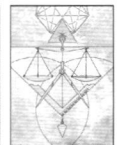

God, the Cause
The Creator of the Universe of Physics

The Prophet
The Channel

Your Higher Goal

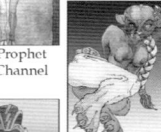

Your Spiritual Teacher

The Wisdom of the Ancestors

Your Higher Self
Your Leading Angel

Your Higher Self
Your Guardian Angel

You the Soul

Biographical Notes

When I talk about how the vision of the deck came to me, perhaps I should better say: *I remember* the images of the cards and the system of the deck, because my memories of the world where this deck is a daily reality are so vivid, and detailed, and coherent, and I have had them such a long time, that I have to accept that the ideas shown here are not the product of my overflowing imagination.

The myth of AboraMana introduced here comes from my home planet which is separated from planet Earth, not by space, but by time. As far as I could understand the explanations when I was recruited for my current mission, planet Earth and my home planet are traveling on the same lane of the time highway—our planet behind Earth. Because Earth is slowing down—for reasons unknown to us, because our planet keeps her timing close to perfect—our planet one day is bound to crash into Earth from behind; again, not in Space/Matter, but in Time. Since I am only a master of history, philosophy, human sciences, and fine arts, I must admit that I have no understanding of time physics; that's why I can't explain it better. Everything I tell you here, I had to take at face value, and I know that the ChairWoman of the GreatCouncil who tongue-lashed me into this mission lies without shame when it suits her purposes.

I was sent to Earth—against my will I need to stress again—for two reasons.

First, I'm supposed to introduce the deck of AboraMana to the human children of planet Earth because, as the ChairWoman explained, the behavior of humans regarding the physical and biological creation of their planet slows planet Earth down far beyond all permissible limits and she hopes that understanding and applying the deck will influence the human behavior to the better, so that the planet can speed up again. According to her, speaking as HighPriestess in Service of AboraMana, human behavior influences the behavior of the planet within the cosmic net—whatever she means by that...

Spoken ExCathedra:
A human's attitudes and ways of acting is based on his thinking and his emotions as the two parts of his mind, and the contents of his mind are influenced by what he believes in. (To believe means: Not known but nevertheless taken for granted.) In other words, a human's believe-system colors and biases the contents of his mind, which form his attitudes, which he expresses in his way of acting.

So if you want to change a human's way of acting, you have to change his believe-system, and this is the open intend of this work, because We can't deny anymore that human attitudes and ways of acting need to be changed.

Yours truly, LilithYggdrasil
HighPriestess in Service of AboraMana

The second reason is that I am to observe the behavior of humans without prejudice or other filters, and to record the observed while living the life of a human male in the western society of the 20th/21st century western time reckoning. As disguise, I wear the mask of being an artist. You might as well call me a spy, except that I'm not undercover and nothing about me is kept secret. I even give you my record to read before my Authorities see it.

On my return, which will happen when my Earth-body dies, I am to submit one copy of the observed to my Authorities, and I will keep one copy for myself etched into my Scroll of Memories. What my Authorities do with my report I don't know.

At present time I'm in the observe/record mode of my mission.

In my world I live in our capital city, AtlantaCaldera, which is divided within the geological and geomantic parameters into Four Quarters, each for one of the Four Elemental Houses: Air, Fire, Water, and Stone. Each quarter has a cathedral for AboraMana, Goddess of Life, Love, and Beauty. Her oldest cathedral is a cave with a pond in the WaterQuarter, the old fishermen's quarter, which is also the quarter where I live when I'm not living on planet Earth.

As a citizen of the WaterQuarter, I honor AboraMana in Her manifestation as Goddess of Life in the House of Water and communicate with Her as LilithAboraMana. By reason of my advanced age, my nearly obsessive love for my Goddess as Lilith AboraMana, and some obvious malfunctions of my time machine back home, I do not remember Her names in the other three Elemental Houses.

Apropos time machine:
That is naturally not its proper name. I just call it so because I can't grasp the acronym it's inventors invented for it.

In my case it is a mighty flotation tank, totally depriving any sensory input—but a zillion colored wires running in and out, and a zillion colored lights flashing on and off, and a zillion sweet little noises humming—as I perceived when I entered the room with that **** machine. Whether I was given drugs to alter my state of mind I do not know; I certainly was given a medicine that emptied my body completely.

And in that lukewarm brine my body floats, ticking along just fine without me, and here I am, in another body, in another world…

…mistake me not—I was beamed into this my Earth-body the moment my Earth-mother's egg opened to one of my Earth-father's seeds. The timing was perfect, I must admit.

I was conceived, carried, and born like any other human on planet Earth. I live the life of a male human being, and my body will die a human being's death, no way out—or better said: The only way out.

Anyway, the deck of cards is the most important of our Holy Scriptures and every person owns at least one deck in one of the many editions painted by different artists throughout the centuries. They are cherished collectibles and the collector's fairs are always overrun. One deck is given by the HighPriestess to every newborn baby at the Ceremony-of-Introduction-Into-Society, starting many a famous collection. We consider the deck as a book of lessons to be learned. Some people use it for divining; children gamble with them for small coins; and in school it is used to clarify the human position in respect to the planet we live on, and in respect of the grand scheme of things in general.

Since I'm a MasterWithoutSeat in the Guild of Artists and Artisans of the WaterQuarter, I was permitted to create my own deck. Within the fast bound rules of the iconography of our Holy Scriptures every artist is free to create whatever he likes.

(Iconography: Visual images with a transcendent or religious meaning. The transcendent meaning, the iconography of the cards is explained in this script.)

For example: The rainbow always symbolizes the spiritual universe; or the heptagon is always the Philosopher's Stone as the concept of the All-including Truth.

To illustrate: A painting of the Goddess as Lilith AboraMana in the House of Water must have an octopus (or sunfish as we call them) somewhere in the picture, because the sunfish is Her holy animal in the House of Water, just as the butterfly or the colibri (humming bird) is Her holy animal in the House of Air, or the scarab in the House of Stone, or the snake in the House of Fire.

For my deck I used many of the sketches I drew when I traveled all the Inner Islands and many of the Outer Islands on government mission. This makes my deck quite unique because, generally speaking, the artists of AtlantaCaldera don't like to travel. They think imagination and reading stories is a substitute for going there and looking for yourself.

Many concepts I show in the deck are well known to humans on Earth because they were channeled from my world to spiritually advanced women and men on Earth hoping to accelerate the planet on the time highway. But to my disappointment I find that many are misunderstood, or wrongly interpreted, or malevolently falsified, by whom and for what reason is unknown to us. (Part of my mission is to find answers to that question.)

To explain what I mean; I'll give you some examples:

The God of the dominant religion on Earth ordered humankind to "subdue" Earth which means *to bring under control using force*. And He also ordered them to "dominate" (*to over-rule*) all life-forms on planet Earth. And the members of the dominant society, influenced by the dominant religion, do exactly that, as everyone can observe; and the sad end of the process of *controlling and dominating using force* is the destruction of Life on Earth.

The dominant religion sees the FirstWoman of their legends as being primarily responsible for all the evil in humankind; and the sad end of this story is the devaluation of womankind in general, resulting in all the evil men did and still do to women; and that causes the destruction of the fabric of human society, as everyone can observe, too.

The dogma of the dominant religion on planet Earth tells humans again and again that they are basically bad because they inherited an original sin; and if you tell good people long enough that they are bad they *become* bad and behave accordingly.

The dogma of the dominant religion on planet Earth tells humans again and again that they are too weak to save themselves by bettering themselves every day and thus they need to believe in a god-like savior to do it for them. And therefore humans give up as pointless this most important human business of life and run their lives in apathy, ignorance, and stupor, pursuing goals as defined by the "profoundly sick society" they live in (Krishnamurti).

Other examples are:

On Earth, created by the Hebrew tradition, Lilith is seen as the first wife of FirstMan Adam, who married FirstWoman Eve when Lilith fled into the desert because she did not want to play the passive role in her relationship with Adam. "...she did not want to lay under him, and he did not want to lay under her...," as the legend intones. (See here, LilitWisdom: Avoiding conflict is the most peaceful form of resistance). Later she became the serpent that gave Eve that infamous apple, and still later she became a children-eating demon and a mother of demons.

The truth is, Lilith is the name of AboraMana as the Firstborn in the House of Water. Lilith means serpent, or snake, as the animal spirit of intuitive wisdom, seen as a feminine quality. It also means deep, as in profound; or deep as the Philippine Trench.

You'll also find that I changed the beloved melody of Air, Fire, Water, *Earth* to the correct form of Air, Fire, Water, *Stone*, because the Elemental Houses were created *before* the creation of Life on this planet. "Earth" is either the name of the planet we live on, or it means soil, or humus, where plants can grow in, and humus contains a lot of plant- and animal-matter, living or dead, and plants and animals are AboraMana's children.

The scientists of Magic understand AboraMana as the Fifth Elemental House, although they see AboraMana as secondary to the original Four Houses because those can exist without AboraMana, but AboraMana cannot exist without them. Some scientists even claim the original Four Houses were created only that AboraMana could build Her House on them.

City people generally say only Lilith when they mean our Goddess. To make things more complicated they say also only Lilith when they mean the ChairWoman of the GreatCouncil, whose title is LilithYggdrasil. (Ygdrasil means Old Tree Roots In Earth And Carries Sky).

Author's Note

Before I started painting the deck and writing this script I wrote down a pretty precise account of the recruiting interview with LilithYggdrasil and the Tribune of AtlantaCaldera, and about the events when the GreatCouncil prepared me for this mission.

Before I knew that somewhere out there in the Atlantic Ocean there was an island called San Miguel de La Palma with the steepest caldera on planet Earth (nine kilometers/5.5 miles diameter and 1,500/5,000 feet meters deep), I had the vision of AtlantaCaldera, exactly the caldera of La Palma halfway submerged in the ocean.

Before I ever imagined myself living in a cave and having my studio in a cave above the Puerto de Tazacorte on La Palma Island, I wrote down the memories of my life in AtlantaCaldera, living with my wife Gallia Heliopola in a cave, in a city of caves in the crater of a volcano.

Before I realized that I was sent here on this mission on planet Earth, I wrote about similar missions in other times and to other places—among others, my memories about my wanderings in Kana'an with JeshuaBenMiriam, aka Jesus Christ.

And, as I painted the first pictures shown in this deck (The Dancers of Air and Fire, Lucifera, the Bitch) I had no idea that I had started a whole deck of cards, and I had no idea how many cards the deck will have in the end. I found out only later, as I was sure the work was finished, when I counted them for the first time. And I didn't paint the cards in any order, I painted them as they flashed into my mind.

And, when I wrote my memoirs about my life in AtlantaCaldera I was living in Frankfurt/Main in Germany as a professional artist but I didn't have the faintest clue about what was the point of my life, except to keep on looking and painting, thinking and writing till I dropped dead. And measured by Earth standards, I was already an old man.

The Tribune of AtlantaCaldera

...in the Name of LilithYggdrasil,
HighPriestess in Service of AboraMana

Declaration of Spiritual War

O Lord, deliver us from hell's great fear and gloom
loose Thou our spirits from the larvae of the tomb
to seek them in their dread abodes without affright
on them we will impose our will: The Law of Light

~Adapted from A. Crowley

We oppose every religion that denies the existence of a Living Goddess as real as the Living God that this religion teaches.

We oppose the idea that humans are born wicked, and that they can't better themselves with their own abilities, but that they need to be saved; and We oppose every creed or religion that teaches to kill and to die for a God leads to Ultimate Bliss.

We oppose the idea that humans were created to subdue Earth and to dominate all Living Beings; that they have no obligation toward the work of the Creators; and that they can do to Creation whatever they like.

We fight this war on the spiritual plane; in the realm of God, and Goddess, and the Host of Heaven; about the definition of the Human Soul; about the meaning of Life as a Human Being; about Life after Death.

We oppose fundamentalists, fanatics, and missionaries.

We fight this war with artistic and intellectual means only.

We fight this war in the spirit of Voltaire who said to the royalties of France:
"Madame, Sire, I think your opinion is wrong but I will defend with my life your right to speak your opinion in public."

The Ray Of Creation

The Basic Layout Using All Cards of the Deck

00—Zero
The All-Including Truth

The Jokers
First Set > Fate
Second Set > Your Fighting Spirit

1st Plane: The Hall of God
The Matrix that is the Human Soul

2nd Plane: The Science of Physics
The Pillars of the Universe and Time

3rd Plane: Magic Physics
The Four Elemental Houses

4th Plane: The Science of Biology
Life—Death /AboraMana

5th Plane: Magic Biology
Devi and Deva

6th Plane: Humankind
FirstWoman and FirstMan

7th Plane: The Temple
Religion and Ceremony

8th Plane: You
Who are You? Define Yourself

Description and Explanation of the Cards

00 — The All-Including Truth

The All-Including Truth, the Absolute Truth
Also called The Diamond of Total Truth, or the ZeroCard.
The Philosopher's Stone as an idea, or as a philosophical concept.
Beyond all questions and answers.
Can be experienced but can't be talked about.
Also, perfect, meticulous, impeccable as concepts of the Absolute.
Also, The SupremeBeing without a personality, without acting, especially not meddling in human affairs.
Some scientists say the SupremeBeing created the Human Soul. Others say the Human Soul is part of the SupremeBeing, or that all Human Souls together *are* the SupremeBeing.
The "Clear Blue Light" in the *Tibetan Book of Death*.
The "Great Emptiness" of Zen seen in the moment of Satori (total enlightenment).

This card is placed above all other cards and stands alone. Whatever you play with the deck, the ZeroCard is set apart on a good visible spot, to always remind you that everything you consider as true is part—only a part—of the All-Including Truth.
The "Diamond of Total Truth" is shown as a heptagon, where every corner is connected with every other corner. That shows the Cosmic Net where every phenomenon is connected to and influ-

ences every other phenomenon. Each of the facets thus formed is one part of the Total Truth—and because it is the All-Including Truth, your beliefs are a part of it, too, as are the beliefs of all your fellow humans.

The small heptagon in the center of the Diamond develops by itself during the process of drawing the Diamond. (Try it. It is a most beautiful meditation.) This is your Private Window through which you look at that part of the Total Truth you can understand and that you consider as true. Every single human has her own private window just like you. Groups of people, like religious congregations or political parties, are united by the congruence of their individual private windows—and all of us look at the same All-Including Truth.

For example, the Mother Church and all of her sects look through the same private window at that facet of the Total Truth that says: Humans are absolutely lost without a Savior, nothing helps except the firm belief in what our Holy Books tell us about Him, no matter how implausible the stories seem to be to the rational human mind.

The card asks you to expand your private window every day a little bit by learning to look without bias through the private windows of others.

Around the Diamond lies the empty space of creation, the White Chaos, the world of fleeting ideas, chains of thought, intuitive daydreams, the fountain every inspired artist draws from, an emotional and mental universe where everything is possible but nothing is materially real.

The square in the circle below it shows the principle of dualism, in which we live on planet Earth and which we can't change. But when we understand the energy of dualism then we learn to love it and to use it to our personal and social advantage as a woman or man, young or old, during the day and in the night, in good days and in bad—in our down-to-earth daily reality.

The setting of the Diamond, the double snail that eats itself, once more shows the constant moving dual world, which always stays the same, even when the outside appearances change.

The rainbow colored stand shows the Ray Of Creation, which starts at the Source and goes on through all planes of creation, till it ends on the human plane, and there it ends at You, which it is the latest and the last level of creation. That means, that you are the youngest child of creation, and that again means, that you need to respect all the plants and animals as our elder sisters and brothers, and all the oceans and mountains as the base where you stand.

The deck does not show below-human levels of creation, no worlds of devils or demons and no hell, because they do not exist as a part of OurGod's and AboraMana's Creation. Our shamanas found by experience, that they are called into existence by humans who believe in them and feed them with their emotional energy.

Contemplation of the ZeroCard can teach you tolerance and compassion, and it can help you to understand and accept the point of view of others even if you don't agree with them.

Also, never use absolutes in your daily talk like *always* and *never*, *everything* and *nothing*, *everybody* and *nobody*, and such.

Source: The card shows one of the sacred instruments on the main altar of AboraMana's oldest cathedral in our capital city. In similar form, it stands on every altar in every chapel, or temple, or church of every creed and sect on our planet. Part of the celebration on holy days always is a lecture about the ZeroCard. That is the reason we never had religious wars and felt entitled to kill, torture, or enslave someone with a different faith.

Crystal and the shell of a double-snail on a stand of colored glass, ca. 90 cm / 36 inches high.

Start of Game

The Jokers

First Set / Fate

Also titled, The Invisible Hands Of Fate

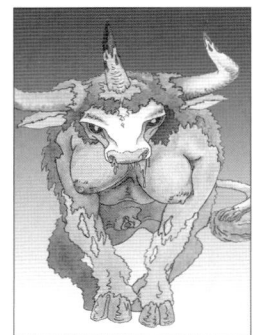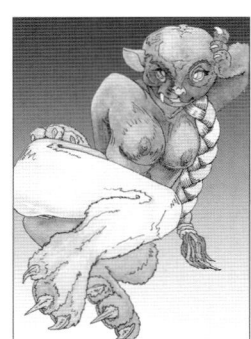

Schicksal in German; literally: That what has been sent to you by Higher Powers. (schicken = to send; sal has its roots in Seele or soul and refers to the spiritual universe).

Kismet in Arab.

According to the old German myth Urd the Spinner, Verdandi the Weaver, and Skuld the Cutter are three ancient sisters dwelling in a cave between the roots of the Tree That Carries The Sky, Yggdrasil. They are older than Gods because, according to the legends and according to all logic, Gods are subject to fate, too.

They are not responsible for the accidents you create because you were driving your car, halfway asleep, running on semi-automatic, listening to your full-blast stereo, arguing with the one next to you, while phoning you'll be late at work because of the infuriating traffic tie up. This is not *Bad Luck*, or the Dictat of Destiny, or something like that; it is your own doing for whatever reason you have, and no matter what justifications you might find to declare yourself innocent, the helpless victim of bad luck.

The Sisters are not Karma because you yourself only are responsible for your Karma, which says, What goes around comes around, which means, Sooner or later you'll receive what you gave. The Sisters symbolize those things in your life you are objectively—in the down-to-earth common reality—not responsible for, called *Good* or *Bad Luck*, and it depends on you how you meet your good or bad luck and thus create your Karma.

Fate works on the material plane only. Being born as a woman is your fate, for example, as is the color of your skin, or your talents. Sometimes it is called destiny; it is that what happens to you in your daily reality and in your life in general, coming at you from the outside.

You are objectively not responsible for your fate but you have to live your fate to the fullest—you have to make do with what you have.

Before you entered your Earth-body, you knew, understood, and agreed on what your fate on planet Earth will be. This is what your Higher Self, or your Angels know about you. But to live the life of a human, you needed to forget that, and now your fate is a complete mystery to you until you realize that whatever *happens* to you is what you agreed on—and that again means that you really can't blame somebody else, or your fate, or your good or bad luck, for the joy and the pain given to you during your life's journey.

A similar approach you can find in the *Tibetan Book Of Death*, where on the Higher Plane after the death of your former body, you are clearly made responsible for the choice of your parents, the gender of your present-time body, the time, and the cultural group you wanted to be born in.

X1 — Urd the Spinner

The Spider on the first card of Fate symbolizes appearance and the gender of your body, the talents, abilities, and special traits of character that have been given to you by the PowersGreaterThanYou, and the Spinner spins all your talents, your experiences, your learned abilities, your knowledge, and your understanding into one strong thread.

The Spinner also symbolizes Endlessness.

X2 — Verdandi the Weaver

The Weaver works you into the fabric of human society. She connects you to people and circumstances you "accidentally" meet and it is up to you how you interact with them, thus creating your Karma. She challenges you to become part of the fabric to make it stronger and more beautiful. The red knots at the top show the people you are very closely connected with.

The rainbow colors of the fabric show you that fate has to be accepted as a gift given to you by the PowersGreaterThanYou to help you to become what you really are. This accepting attitude for a heavy burden of fate makes it easier to carry.

X3 — Skuld the Cutter

The Cutter represents Things Done or a Thread Of Fate Fulfilled. Giving birth is cutting loose for both the mother and the child, for example.

She lets you end one thread of your fate to make you free for another thread. This new beginning is shown by the rising sun in the lower right corner.

She does not mean the death of your material body; she symbolizes the death of your fixed pre-concepts and prejudices; she also means letting go of people and of possessions; and she helps you to accept what you consider as a heavy loss.

The Jokers

Second Set — The WarriorGoddess

Literally: The Goddess Of The Warriors

They show your fighting spirit and your sense of competition. Don't fearing opposition.

You need to know your goal, or what you want to achieve, before you can apply these four cardinal virtues in a sensible way, otherwise your are just a "loose cannon," out of control of yourself, a danger to your fellow human beings.

Also, action with the goal to stop an aggressor's aggression. The action varies from mild to extreme violence, as the occasion demands.

Stand up for your rights when they are denied to you, but avoid over-reaction to imagined aggression.

Y1 — Recklessness

Recklessness (shown as Gryffa here) is a warrior-energy not only directed against others but also, mainly, against yourself.

Not caring what happens to oneself on the way to a clearly defined goal; being prepared to accept personal disadvantages and discomforts to reach that goal. JeshuaBenMiriam, aka Jesus Christ, is an extreme example.

Recklessness is sometimes called "controlled madness." One example of recklessness is found in the mental state of the feared berserkers of the ancient Nordic warrior culture. They were able to crank themselves into such a controlled madness that they attacked naked, with only their swords, far in front of their own lines, the battle line of the enemy, not caring what happened to themselves.

Y2 — Flexibility

Flexibility (shown as Kentoura here) is like water running around rocks on its way to the ocean, always searching for the easiest way out. Easy doesn't mean cheap, fast, and ugly. It means the most economic means to reach a goal without sacrificing good workmanship and beauty.

Being able to change routines and old ways of doing things; being creative in your thinking and actions.

Finding fast new ways of attack and defense.

Fast body, mental, and emotional reactions.

In certain situations avoiding conflicts can be part of flexibility. Lilith, the first wife of Adam, as she ran away because she didn't want to be dominated by Adam, is a good example.

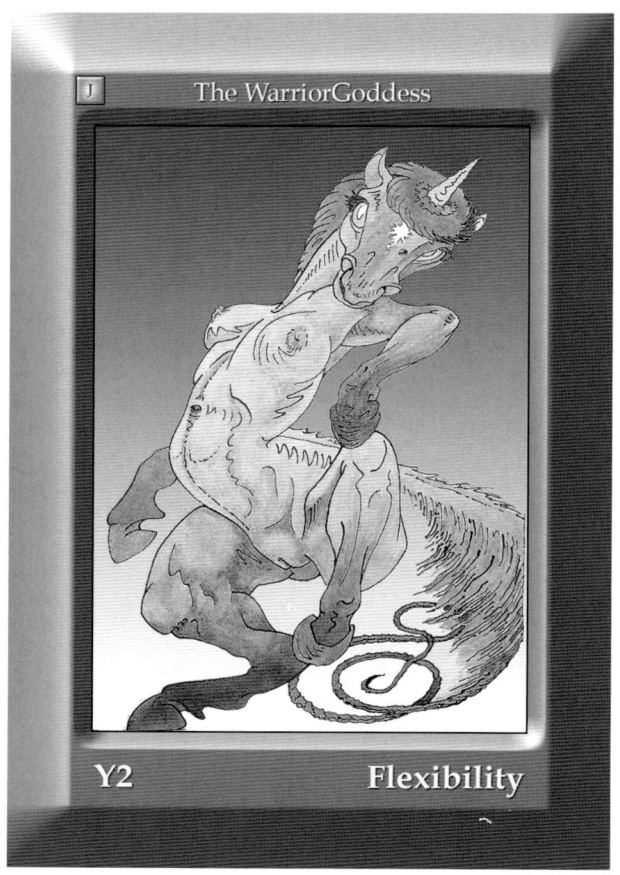

Y3 — Perseverance

Perseverance (shown as Minataura here) is like the steady drop that wears a hole in a stone.

Perseverance is not being stubborn or clinging to old habits. Perseverance needs a clearly defined and reachable goal to focus on.

Never giving in, remaining firm under pressure.

Consistency; steady and continued actions over a long period of time despite difficulties and setbacks.

Also, burning the bridges you crossed; never looking back.

A certain kind of tunnel vision can be part of it, too—to give so much importance to reaching your goal that everything else, including your own present-day life, becomes trivial because you invest everything you have in reaching your goal.

The battle cry of the Spanish conquistadores in the Americas: Victory or death!

To continue to fight the war although a battle is lost.

Y4 – Patience

Patience (shown as Sphinga here) is the ability to wait and endure without falling into apathy.

Patience is not passive waiting for an opportunity to change a situation to your own advantage but very attentive observation of the situation with the constant readiness to interfere when the opportunity offers itself.

History: The WarriorGoddess is very old, on the Inner Islands she has no sanctuaries anymore; on the Outer Islands of the Barbarians, she is still worshiped but she looses more and more of her powers because of the civilizing influence of AtlantaCaldera. Today, students of martial art use the four aspects of her as sign, seal, and symbol of their order.

The WarriorGoddess is not the Goddess Of War because the horrors of war is a human creation, but not the responsibility of a PowerGreaterThanUs. On planet Earth people often say or write, "The war broke out," as if it was like a volcano breaking out, or a tsunami rolling over helpless humans. A war never, ever "breaks out." Wars are always consciously and willfully started by humans.

Some studies claim that they also represent the Three Pillars of the Universe and Time. The most accepted order is: Gryffa = Space, Kentoura = Energy, Minataura = Matter, Sphinga = Time.

Source: Copy of the only complete set of an antique deck in our central library. Woodcut, light ink-wash on card paper. Time of origin unknown, not dated, no signature.

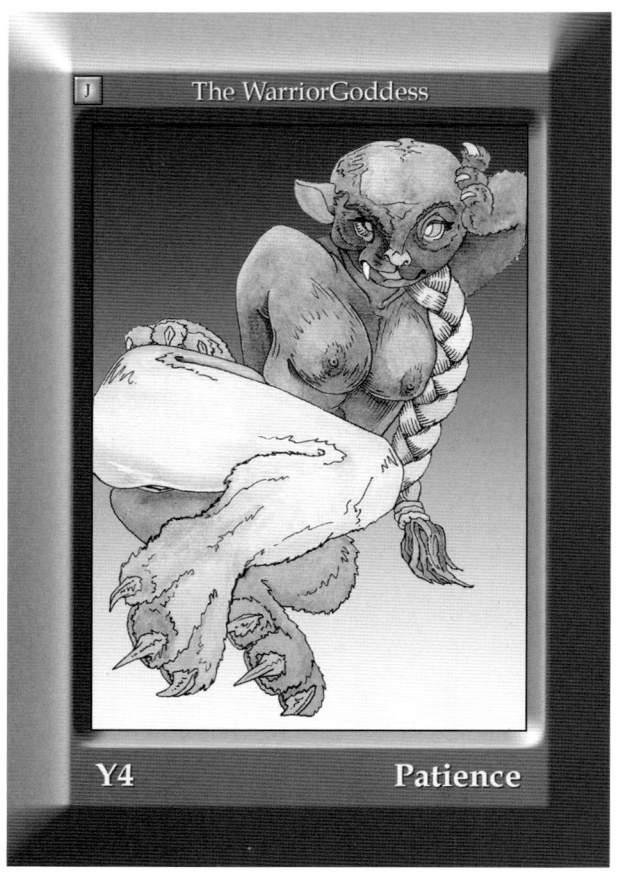

The 1st Plane of The Ray of Creation

The Hall of God

The Matrix that is the Human Soul

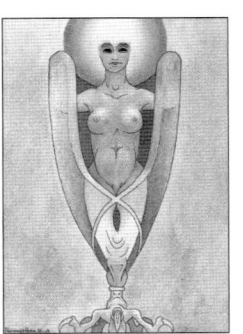
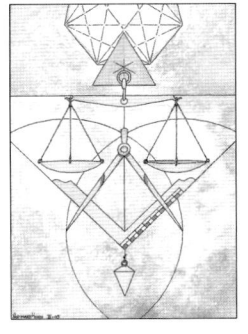
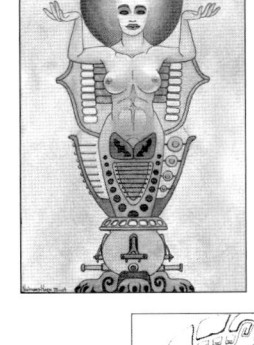

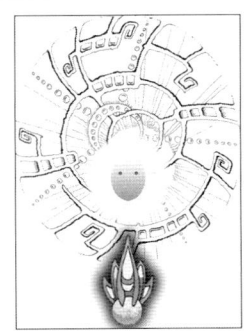

Since we talk about God, we have to talk about religion.

To tell a story you have to invent persons that act out the story. Persons have limitations in their mental structure called Blind Spot. Without blind spots on the side of the actors, no story would be possible because every story revolves around problems created by blind spots, and the solution of the problems. All-mightiness and All-knowledge don't allow for problems because there is no blind spot, so there is no need to act to find a solution to a problem caused by a blind spot, so there is no story to tell.

As it is said in the Scriptures: In the beginning was the Word, which means, in the beginning was a story; and all stories are constructs of the human mind.

Humans on planet Earth, no matter at what time or of what creed, tell each other stories about Gods and/or Goddesses and/or other members of the spiritual universe interacting with humans in their daily lives. If you tell a story often enough, it solidifies and becomes more and more a Truth-of-Reality for the people who tell the story and for those who listen to that story. And slowly, the story becomes a Holy Scripture unshakably true; and a lot of scholars find their daily bread by interpreting the story and proving that the story is true (or not true).

Around this mentally created solid reality humans build rituals and ceremonies, arts and crafts, and a caste of priests, and a so-called religion emerges out of nowhere and occupies large areas in the mental space of a believer.

It is also the habit of humans to see their particular God as the One-And-Only-True-God because they don't understand that they look through their comparatively small private window at the infinite All-Including Truth. This is particularly true for the monotheistic religions. There *is* a SupremeBeing independent of humans which is not a construct of a human mind, there is no doubt about that, but it says, "Can be experienced, but can't be talked about." When humans forget that they "can't talk about It" and start adorning the SupremeBeing with human traits, acting out stories like humans would, they leave the realm of the SupremeBeing and enter the realm of Goddesses and Gods.

Since Gods/Goddesses are a creation of the human mind—even when they are inspired by PowersGreaterThanUs—they are finite and depend on their believers. Prosperous believers make prosperous Gods—with the disappearance of the last believer, the God dies, or at least goes into hibernation. That happened to SunGod Ra, GodFather Wotan, MoonGoddess Selene, LoveGoddess Aphrodite, and many others.

Besides other Goddesses and Gods living in other major cultures, the only survivors in the battle of the Gods, acted out by their believers, are the Hebrew-Christian God and the Muslim God. Moshes Hebrew God is still going pretty strong, because He draws strength out of the alias He planted into the Christian God image.

As said before, the more devoted believers a God has, the stronger He grows and thus a strong God gives more of His strength to the believers. Moshes God YWHW didn't wipe out the Goddesses and Gods of Kana'an because He was a so much nicer guy but because His believers were a highly trained and armed killer-force with nothing equal in far sight, driven and pushed ahead by "OurGod and His Prophet Moshe Said So!"

The Christian God did not win the battle over most other Gods all over the planet, and achieved a pretty dangerous stale mate with the Muslim God because He was so much more true than all the other

Gods, but because His believers always had the better weapons for the dissemination of The Word, and they were always eager to use them for their God against His enemies because "God Said So!" and don't be mistaken, they truly believed it.

There are two kinds of Gods, there are the Old Gods and there are the New Gods. The Old Gods are the Gods and Goddesses of nature, which means the female and the male aspects are pretty well balanced. They represent forces of nature like moon, or sun, or rain, or volcanoes, or death, or fertility, or human experiences and facts of life like love, and joy, and sorrow, etc.

AboraMana is an Old Goddess, in fact, She is the oldest because She represents Life and all individual life-forms on planet Earth.

Moshes God is the oldest of the New Gods—his God is the source of the Christian God and the source of the Muslim God, although both hate to admit that. Contrarily, both did their best to wipe out the believers of the God YWHW.

Moshe tried to invent an abstract God. But humans are visual beings, they need and they love and they always make images that represent That-Which-Is-Without-Image. This is an un-erasable part of the religion-matrix in the emotional body of humans.

Moshe made his God purely male, with not a fraction of female, although humans live in the dual world of woman and man, and they know it, and they basically love it.

Moshe's God runs a tight ship, just like Moshe had to run a tight ship as he transformed the Children of Israel from an unruly mob of shepherds into the strongest fighting army of that time, consisting of a nation on the move, armed to the teeth, united by One God and God's Only True Prophet Moshe, and the people have a common goal to achieve in the Name of God under the leadership of Moshe. Moshe's God joins forces with Moshe the Prophet, which makes the job of Moshe the Leader so much easier.

Since all Gods are constructs of the human mind, the understanding of the character of the God is the key to understanding the character of the human who believes in Him. And, since the God of a believer is as real to the believer as the believer is real to himself, the God's character re-enforces the character of the believer; the God and the believer both re-enforce each other until the combined forces of a human and his God are strong enough to turn objective Wrong into Right because "God Said So!" as it was done during the times of the inquisition, only for one example.

(Objective wrong is a transgression against the first law of social behavior. Don't give what you don't want for yourself.)

The more you believe in a God, the more real He becomes to you, and your God does exactly what you believe Him to do—true belief is a tremendous creative energy with the ability to turn emotional and mental images into three-dimensional solid things and into materially relevant actions.

Your God becomes what you believe him to be. You believe in a God outside of you and He'll be outside of you. You believe Him violent, He will be violent. You believe that He will punish you or reward you according to your conduct in life, He will punish you or reward you. He becomes and is whatever you believe Him into; and if you don't believe in a God, than no God exists except in the "superstitious" mind of others. And if you like, you can dream up your own God or Goddess, too, nothing wrong with that because all Gods are small facets of the All-Including Truth.

This footnote to my Authorities is completely hidden to humans on planet Earth. We call them Blind Believers and consider them as pretty dangerous.

There is nothing wrong with believing in Goddesses and Gods as a Seeing Believer, which means, *Knowing* that every God is an artificial creation of the human mind, no matter what the priests of the God claim. Contrarily, believing in a Spiritual Universe including Gods and Goddesses, and a Host of Heaven enriches the emotional life of humans and their societies through all the times by transforming the belief into works of visual arts and music, solemn rituals and colorful ceremonies, and it serves as a focus on a common effort not for self-celebration, but for celebration of something, or someone, greater than ourselves.

Choosing one God or Goddess out of many as a focus for your wish to honor the PowersGreaterThanYou, for a human never to comprehend, is a free decision, which means there can't be a wrong decision.

The question is only: Which of the available Gods/Goddesses and the systems the believers built around them in times past allow for a:

Human Being
Most Beloved Being
Self Aware
Aware of Life and Death
Aware of Good and Evil
Given Free Decision
Hologram of the SupremeBeing
???

All stories about the interaction of Goddesses/Gods and the Host of Heaven with humans are told to explain the world and the human position in it, with the open or hidden intent of the tellers and interpreters, the priests and preachers, to influence the mind and thus the life of the individual, including the individual's conduct within society.

So here is another story.

01 – God – The Big Bang

Not the SupremeBeing as defined in the ZeroCard.

The creator of the Universe of Physics: Space, Matter, Energy, and secondary Time as a result of the interaction of the three, i.e., planet Earth without Biological Life, within the solar system, and as far out as we can reach with our instruments.

The energy that keeps the galaxies, suns, planets, moons, comets, and all that spinning and burning and sparkling.

The creative energy of the analytical mind, perceived as a male person with personal characteristics and traits. He is the cool engineer, the precise calculator, the builder, the mason.

Some sects call this God by the Name of Abbadam. That is the shortening of Abba Adam. It means "Father of Adam," (Abba = Father, in the sense of Daddy) because the analytical mind of humans is considered a male energy.

The card is also called "The Big Bang" as a concession to the scientific point of view. But whenever you ask the scientist: *Who* made

the Big Bang? And *what* did bang big? he doesn't know the answer, but comes with the promise that sooner or later he'll find out.

Some humans call it Intelligent Design. Those words are probably used to avoid the word God, because the word "God" is occupied by the Hebrew-Christian God. But if it makes sense for you, why not, provided you keep in mind that AboraMana could be called the Intelligent Designer of all Living Beings.

But we don't really care how our cosmos came into existence, because we think it is not important to find out what actually happened, but it is very important to us that through Life, through AboraMana, the cool engineer learned how to love. Through the love of AboraMana. He became the All-Loving Father, according to the Confirmation of our Creed: "The Love of GodFather and the Love of GoddessMother hold together the whole universe, and Their Love is the only Driving Power of Life on planet Earth."

Some sects honor Him also as the creator of the energy of biological life. But our scientists of the divine haven't found out yet whether God blew His odem consciously and with full intent into the primordial soup and thus created Life, i.e., AboraMana; or whether the primordial soup sucked the spark of life out of God without His own intent, maybe even against His will, and thus created Life out itself.

This card asks you to become and stay aware of the difference between:

God's creation (the universe of physics),

AboraMana's creation (the universe of biology),

The creation of humans, divided in two manifestations: Arts, and technology for improving God's/Goddess' creation, including the offal they produce while improving).

The card shows the Diamond of Total Truth behind the male triangle of God. That means that this God is—like every other God—part of the All-Including Truth.

Below the triangle we see the tools necessary to build and construct a universe, be it a house or a cosmos: The scale is the moving female horizontal line and the plumb is the static male vertical line. The scale also shows the perfectly balanced dualism we live in on the material plane, and on the mental plane it shows the sacred gift of free decision without hope of reward or fear of punishment.

The dualism of the scale is repeated in the compass, where one point holds the center and the other point draws the circle. The holding point is female because it is static, and the drawing point is male because it is moving, which shows that every positive male activity is motivated by female energy. The scale with the plumb and the compass apparently contradict each other, but this is just another quirk of the dual principle.

The right angle with the measurements is the perfect instrument to divide a circle into four equal parts, which are also the four quarters of our planet's surface. The four right angles are male and active, and they divide the perfect circle, which is female and passive.

Source: Label of the *Book of Geometrics* used in our public schools.

The Glory of God

The Three Holy Sisters

---

02 — Serapha — Light

Light, endless cosmic energy.
In the human mind it is objectivity, impartiality.
Seeing with the third eye, being able to visualize what exists but can't be seen with the material eyes.
(To visualize is the process of building a three-dimensional moving color picture in your mind and to hold it there as long as you want.)
Seeing with the material eyes, being able to see the visible world as abstract patterns, and color patches, and flat forms without meaning.
Seeing without naming, or assuming, or interpreting, or explaining the seen.
This ability is important for objectivity. It can and should be trained, especially by visual artists, but is a rewarding ability for everyone, because it inhibits pre-concepts and helps you to see things as they really are.

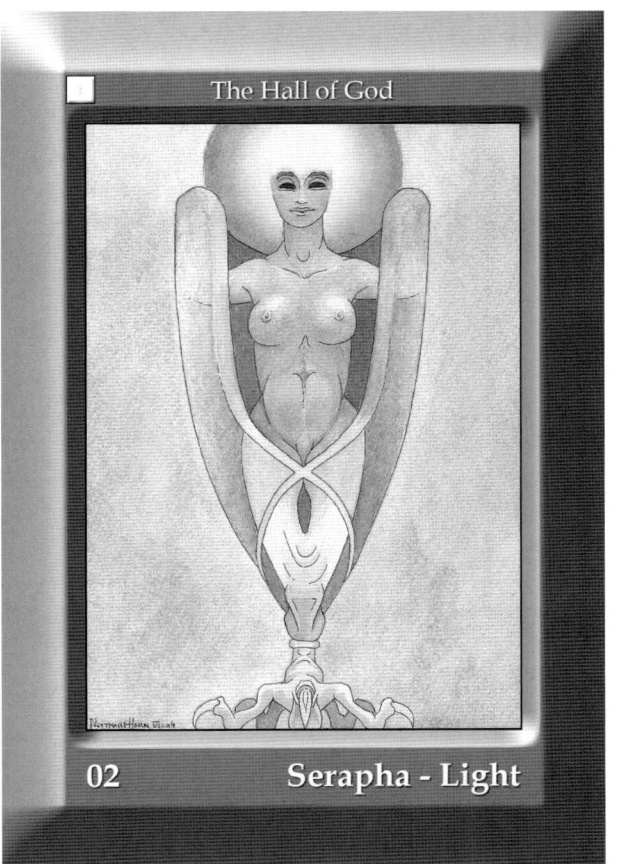

Serapha pairs with Cheruba in the set: Know ThySelf on the 8th Plane, asking: *Is your attention more on looking?*

Serapha has a halo in the colors of the day, her half sister, Cheruba, has a halo in the colors of the night, both together show the rainbow, the spectrum of colors visible to the human eye. The colors of the rainbow are a mystical energy, manifest on the solid material plane for everyone to see. You can touch the rain, the sunlight touches you, but you can't touch the rainbow and there is not one human being who is not moved at the sight of a rainbow. (Throughout the deck the rainbow symbolizes the spiritual universe, the realm of the Host of Heaven, the world of angels, power animals, spiritual leaders, advanced masters, etc.)

The legend tells that God dedicated His rainbow to His most beloved AboraMana, when He, for the first time, heard a Humpback Whale singing.

Source: Light on the main altar in Lilith AboraMana's cathedral, AtlantaCaldera. Translucent glass, gold, ca 75 cm / 30 inches high.

03 — Cheruba — Sound

Sound, lit.: Songs of nature.
 Listen to the emotional contents of the words spoken.
Listen with your material ears.
Listen with your third ear by listening to the sounds of nature and finding rhythm and melody in it.
Also, music, which is structured sound made by humans.
She is also abused as noise made by man which is not music.
Pairs with Serapha for the set: Know ThySelf on the 8th Plane, asking: *Is your attention more on listening?*

The legend tells: Without God's planning or knowing, Cheruba came into existence, when He created the Three Pillars of the Universe, (energy, matter, space) because it is a law of creation. "When energy drives matter through space sound will come into existence." You can verify this law when you sit on the beach and you observe the energy of the wind pushing the water through the space from the horizon towards you, and you will hear the sound of the breaking waves.

Cheruba has two parts. One part comes out of the universe of physics, the other comes from the universe of AboraMana because of Her overflowing joy of life.

The legend tells: "When AboraMana created the living beings, She taught Her children to sing, and since then all living beings sing Prayers of Thanx to their Mother, and the Goddess of Life dedicated the songs of Her children to Her Father, the Father of Her children."

Serapha and Cheruba, later AboraMana, belong to the race of beings that are one and many at the same time. Their eyes are black, because they see the unveiled Total Truth.

Source: Musical instrument in the monastery on the Island of Mo'orea. Different materials, ca. 30 m / 100 feet high

The nuns and monks of the monastery built this instrument on the front platform of their temple, which stands high above the sea on a ridge between two valleys. They built funnels into the valleys where they open to the ocean and connected the funnels through long pipes with the copper kettle on the lower part of he instrument. The mostly onshore wind is funneled into the instrument, where it produces so-called natural vibrations, and when the wind is right you can hear a very complex music of natural vibrations far out over the sea, and the steep, fairly smooth cliff behind the temple doubles the effect with it's echo. In fact, when I visited Mo'orea on government mission, I heard the Cheruba long before I could see the island.

To clarify a point, the nuns and monks of Mo'orea love Abora-Mana just as much as anybody else on our planet, and since She is the Goddess of Love, they never practiced celibacy which they consider as one of the most silly notions that can cross the mind of a bodily, mentally and emotionally healthy woman or man. Contrarily, Tantra is one of their religious practices. They are called nuns and monks because they live in a closed compound under pretty strict rules, and they devote their lives to the praise of AboraMana, the search for the Philosophers Stone, and the maintenance of the Cheruba.

It is known that J. S. Bach was closely connected to the Cheruba of Mo'orea, and every musician worth his salt can tap into her.

04 — Lucifera — Speak Truth

Bearer of Light, Messenger of Truth.
The spoken word.
Also, *listen* to the spoken word.
Speak free. Also, speak truth and teach.
Speaking free without love creates hard feelings.
Speaking the truth without love destroys the willingness of the other to learn and to understand.
Also, walk what you talk, or live what you preach.
Also, on the negative side, stupidity, which is having little knowledge and experience without realizing it; and it is the inability to listen and the unwillingness to learn. Part of stupidity is self-righteousness: I'm right and you are wrong, end of story!

Lucifera was created *after* the creation of humankind. She is sent to us to teach us about the Light. Her golden mask with the twisted horns shows the twisted minds of the unenlightened, but she promises that the horns and the minds will straighten out with each step towards enlightenment. In her left hand she carries the Diamond of

Total Truth, in her right hand she carries a vessel with the symbol of flames, which contains scrolls with lectures on the technology how to see the All-Including Truth. In her golden racing boots she hurries through all levels of consciousness and offers the word of truth to every sentient being for the taking. Her eyes are closed so she can't see you, which means: She offers the word of truth to every human being, no matter what color, gender, or creed, you just have to grab for it and take it.

The background shows a sunlit clearing in a forest to remind you that you can meet her on unexpected places, not only in books, or temples, or monasteries, when you are alert and look with clear eyes at the world around you.

She is another example of the twisted truth on planet Earth. First she became the male God Pan with an endless sex-drive, then Hell's Devil with horns and cloven hooves, and totally malevolent intentions towards humankind. But she is truly the bearer of the Divine Light and the teacher on the path to enlightenment.

Lucifera sent all the great and small spiritual teachers to planet Earth. She is also the patron saint of shamanas and kahunas and of all those who heal minds, that's why the saying goes: "The truth will set you free," and "the truth might hurt but it will heal you."

Lucifera helps you to overcome spiritual arrogance because she helps you to understand that every human stands somewhere on the ladder to enlightenment, and always there are some humans climbing up below you (your students) and some humans climbing up above you (your teachers), no matter how far you have climbed until now. She teaches you the humbleness of the masters.

Source: Mural in the hall of ceremonies of the Black Mantilla Sect in the StoneQuarter of AtlantaCaldera. Ca. 3.60 m / 12 feet high. Restored by the author before he left home.

The Madre of the Black Mantilla Sect has a vessel with the flame symbol in her treasury and told me when I visited her on government mission that it was brought to her by LuciferaInPerson. The vessel, she claims, contains lectures on the technologies how to see the Total Truth. On my request to see the vessel she refused with the reasoning I couldn't see it anyway. The Madre channeled with Lucifera's permission part of the teachings to the first Japanese Zen masters, who since then teach sitting Zen and use the vessel with the flame symbol as crown on their pagodas.

But sitting Zen is only one of the many technologies, the Madre said. Counting the beads of a rosary, chanting Hare Krishna, or the spinning of the dervish belong to the same set of technologies to see the Total Truth. She said that Zen is considered the noblest of all technologies, because it is free of religion and any kind of belief, except the belief that it is possible for every human being to find the Philosopher's Stone, called total enlightenment—but you have to go there and practice yourself.

05 — Your Spiritual Master

Your most beloved spiritual teacher.

This card goes with "05 – Serapha In Action" because she is the Driving Angel behind every spiritual master, no matter in what culture he has his roots. They serve the same goal. Serapha is a spiritual drive, fed by an intuitive knowledge of what is right or wrong and a deep compassion for an utterly lost human kind, which possesses the master during his lifetime in a human body on planet Earth, no matter how far he was elevated by his disciples to a god. You know his name if you have one; if you don't have one, go and search for one. There are plenty of them, major ones and minor, and all are equally true. Through the study of spiritual masters, you will find what is true for you.

You can change your master as often as you want to, no harm done; it is part of your search. A spiritual master is like a magnifying glass that makes one facet of the Diamond Of Total Truth visible and understandable. He can't show you the truth, or the validity of his teachings; he can only lead you, and you need to follow him that you

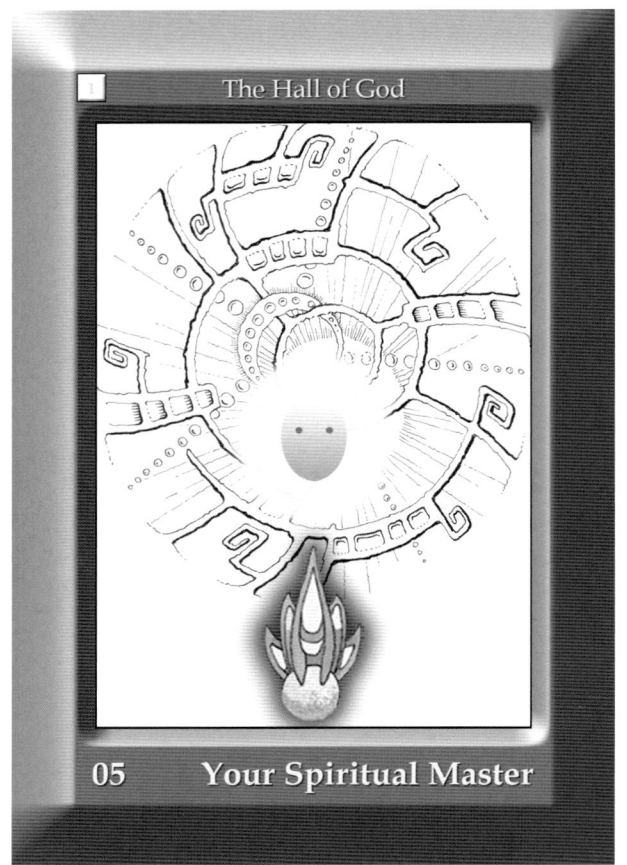

see and understand the truth and validity of his teachings for yourself; and once you see it, you'll be possessed by Serapha, too.

The card says: Follow your master. Don't rest until you are a master yourself and don't need a master anymore. And, do as your master tells you to do. Face, and admit, and shed your justifications for not doing as he says. It also says, listen to the master and not to the preacherman who interprets the master. It also means, don't forget to look without bias and prejudices at the spiritual master of others. Maybe you learn something new, which means you expand your spiritual private window, or now you can look at two or three facets of the Diamond at the same time. Remember: The ultimate goal is seeing The Total Truth, not only some facets.

The card shows at the bottom the flame ball of the pure teachings; the egg-shape above are the faces and the names of all your spiritual teachers, in the past and yet to be met. That also includes all teachers who impressed themselves on your mind during your formative years and thus helped to form your personality as it is today.

The egg-shape here is also used as the symbol for the Source of Life, or The Source in general.

The abstract pattern in the background is the answer to the question you asked your master. Without his explanation his world has no meaning for you.

05 — Serapha in Action

To serve a higher goal.

The legend tells: When people forgot whom they owe their lives and existence, God created a new title and new duties for Serapha, "Defense of the Honor and the Work of The Creators." She joins forces with Lucifera and acts as her body guard.

She is the light that moves freely through all levels of consciousness. This is shown by the rainbow colors on the top of the card, which symbolize the universe of the spiritual worlds. The spiral, the smoke, and the floating spheres in the lower part of the card show the material plane, on which we, as spiritual beings in a material body, live. With the never sleeping eyes on her wings she observes the behavior of humankind and inspires the enlightened ones to try to stop disrespectful behavior of others for the Creation of the Mother-of-Life and the Father-of-the-Universe.

Source: Adapted from a sculpture that crowns a banner for processions in honor of AboraMana. Ca. 30 cm / 12 inches diameter. Photo of the sculpture in possession of the author.

Later we'll talk about the other two members of the Host of Heaven, your Leading and your Guardian Angel, when we explain how we see you on the 8th Plane.

The 2nd Plane of The Ray of Creation

The Science of Physics

The Pillars of the Universe

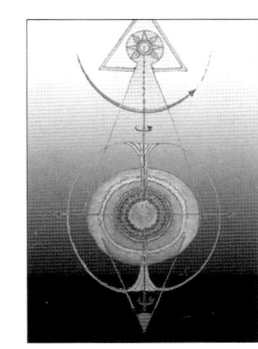
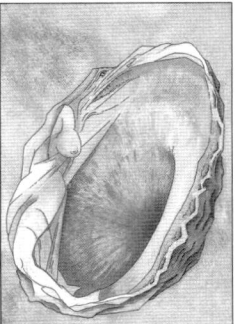

06 — Planet Earth Stage One

Earth: lit. The planet we live on.

In La Lingua Galaktica, every planet that holds human life is called Earth—in their different languages and scripts, of course. Beings are humans when they are social, are aware of death, are aware of good and evil, and enjoy freedom of decision, no matter how funny their bodies might look in your eyes.

Earth also means soil where plants can grow in, i.e., humus or mother earth, in contrast to bare rocks or the sterile sand of the beach.

The "Knowledge of Planet Earth" as it is taught in our primary schools:

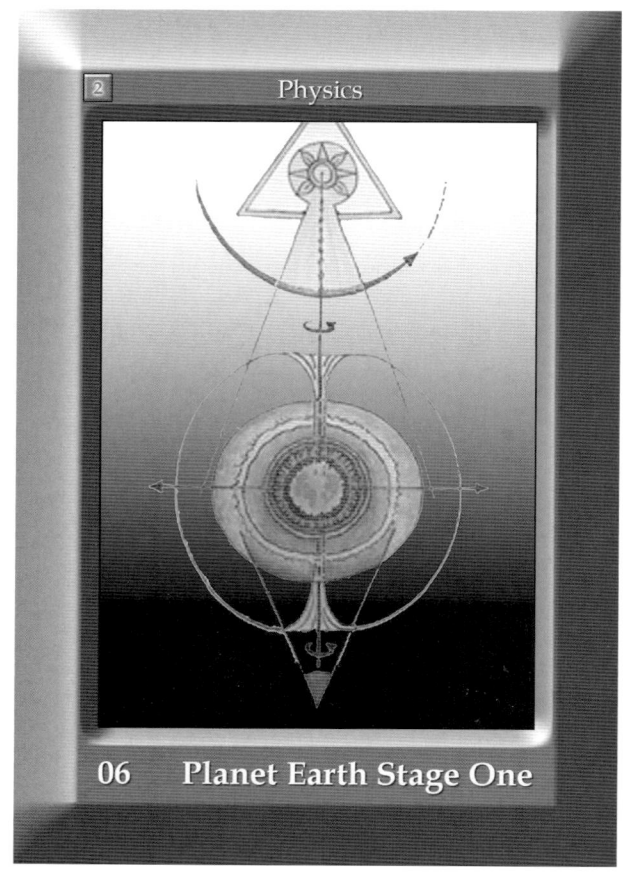

The layers of planet Earth from center to outside are:
Fire—Stone—Water—Air—Magnetic Field.
Between fire and stone is ashes.
Between stone and water is mud.
Between water and air is vapor (steam and clouds).
Above air is nothing (or emptiness, or space).
The magnetic field permeates all.

The poles are the entrance and exit points of the magnetic energy into and out of the planet's body. There the field is densest. Along the equator the field is furthest spread out and therefore weakest. Science agreed to call the North Pole positive and the South Pole negative and that in our era the magnetic stream runs from north to south. On most planets the magnetic poles are close to the geographic poles, but seldom at the same spot, and the magnetic poles are not static in one spot but move about, sometimes as much as fifty miles in a day.

The magnetic field comes into existence through the rotation of the planet and through the friction between the four layers.

The friction between the layers is caused by the different speeds of rotation of the layers.

The different speed of rotation of the layers is caused by the different density of the layers.

The rotation of our planet is caused by an outside energy.

Because our planet rotates in empty space, there is no friction and because of that, the planet potentially rotates in all eternity.

But:

Although God took good care of the lubrication between the layers to create as much magnetic energy as possible, there is still friction that slows down the speed of rotation of the planet. This is the effect of time.

At this stage of creation, planet Earth is a perfect sphere with no wrinkles or protrusions, therefore there are no disturbances in the layers. The boiling fire in the center is safely contained by the layer of stone, the layer of water holds together the layer of stone by adding pressure. There are no currents in the layer of water, no storms in the layer of air, except those caused by the spinning of the planet. The poles and the equator are perfectly aligned to the sun. The magnetic poles sit exactly on the geographic poles and they don't move about. With very little wobble, the planet runs in a nearly perfect circle around the sun. There is no moon. Everything is balanced and in perfect equilibrium.

The law of chaos says that where everything is balanced and in harmony, there is no change. Change occurs only when harmony is upset.

The Pillars of the Universe

Space, Matter, Energy

The legends describe the Three Pillars of the Universe as Titanas, which means:

1. They are a direct creation of God out of Himself (during the Big Bang if you prefer that expression).

2. They are nearly as old as God and they will be the last ones to die when the universe dissolves.

3. They are seen as sex-less pre-life women, because sex came into being much later with the rising of AboraMana.

4. They are incredibly strong—they hold our world into the light and they should be treated with respect.

According to the legends, God first created space as the three-dimensional field to play in, then He created matter to have something to play with. Then He created energy to start and continue the game. Science claims He probably created all together at the same time, while others claim He created energy first. But who really knows?

Source: Triangular monument in the plains of Mara. Concrete, transparent, and translucent glass, ca. 27 m / 90 feet high, each side of the triangle ca. 10 m / 35 feet wide.

The three concrete frames form a triangle that is open on top. It is not possible to enter the inside of the triangle, so nobody knows what is inside, and nobody knows when the monument was built. When I visited Mara on government mission, I sat down with my drawing tools to take a picture of the monument. I soon found that the columns of the frames lean slightly inward and thus create the impression that they are much higher than they actually are. The monument stands on a lonely grassy hill, shaped like a regular, very low-angled cone, and that enhances the illusion of grandeur.

The cards show the labels of the first three lectures on the subject of physics in our public schools.

07 – Space

The Elemental House of Air.
Length, Width, Height.
The circle and the square for a flat universe. Plans, charts and maps. Geometry, trigonometry.
Also: The Squaring of the Circle, or the Circling of the Square.
The empty cube, the hollow sphere for a three dimensional universe.
Limitation, because it is a law of creation: Space must be limited to be a space.
It also means: Out-of-game.
Space is the field you play your games in, like soccer or tennis. To play a game, you first must create a field in which to play, and then you have to give and enforce the first law of the field: Over the boundaries of the field is out-of-game.

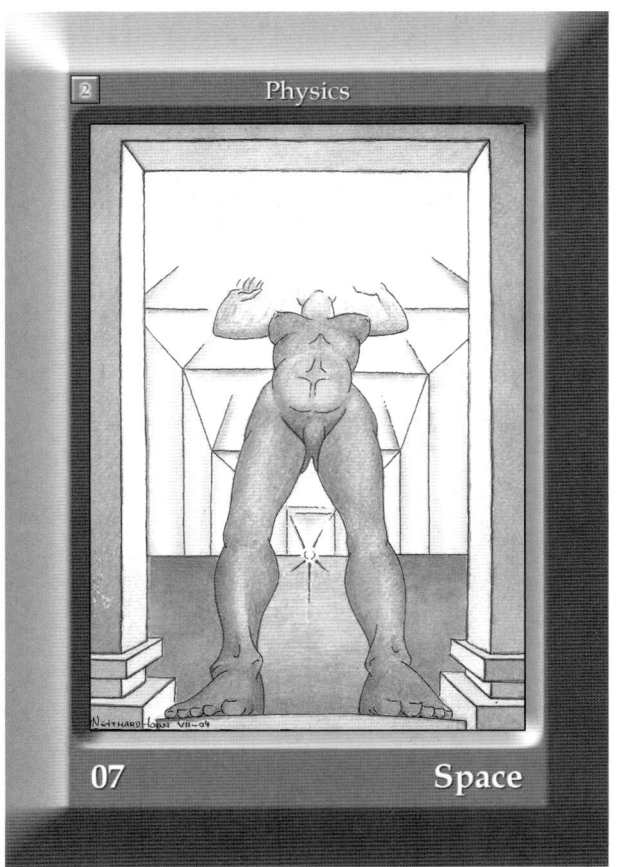

08 — Matter

The Elemental House of Stone.
Gases, Liquids, Solid Matter.
Passive, being driven.
Transition. The question where the one ends and the other begins.

Chaos. (See card 48—Lilith ChaosGoddess. She dwells in the mud, in the transition-zone from wet to dry and not even She can say where wet ends and dry begins.)

The background of the card shows the three different matters of the planet—liquids, solid matters, and gases. They need their sister energy to interact with each other, and in the center of the card you find the central point of perspective from her sister space.

09 – Energy

The Elemental House of Fire.

Magnetic plus/minus energy, static and kinetic gravity, static and kinetic electricity, centrifugal forces. Heat and light as two distinct different forms of energy.

Think about the energies you need to satisfy your daily needs. Think about renewable energy-sources. Think about how to cut down your daily needs.

Active, driving force.

10 – Time

The Elemental House of Water

Our legends tell: God did not *create* time because time is the result of the interaction of matter/space/energy. Time, like sound, is a secondary effect of the creation of matter/space/energy because it is a law of creation: When energy drives matter through space, time is created. This cosmic law is clearly visible on analog watches where the energy of the spring or battery drives the matter of the hands through the space above the face of the clock.

The interaction of the Titanas that creates time also generates Cheruba/sound as time's secondary power. That is why music and time are closely related. They obey the same basic law of metaphysics. The rhythm of music is the passing of time you can hear, like the ticking of old fashioned clocks, but less mechanical. J. S. Bach's Toccata and Fugue in D-Minor is one of the best examples, especially the Fugue.

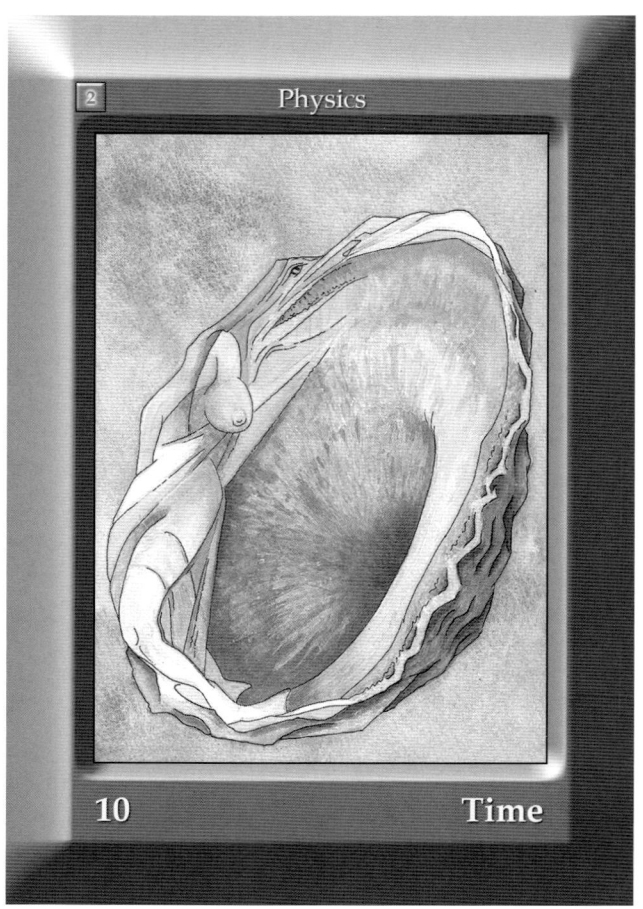

During a public dispute about theological questions on the steps of AboraMana's cathedral in AtlantaCaldera, I once heard the grandmaster of the spiritual philosophers claim:

The Almighty God didn't know that the cosmic law of time being the consequence of the interaction of matter/space/energy exists, otherwise He would have known that He gets Himself into a lot of trouble with the creation of the universe of physics, including His own finiteness. Thus, the master claimed, the Almighty God didn't see the All-Including Truth when He created the universe, and committed, so to speak, spiritual suicide, because He wasn't almighty anymore and finite.

But the HighPriestess, in her usual snotty way, commented on that only: He knew very well what He was doing; He was just bored and created Himself a toy to juggle with and keep spinning—a therapy for a bored God. And, she continued: If He, because of the effects of Time would see His end coming, He could dissolve His creation with a snap of his fingers and be eternal again, no problem. But then He has no longer has a toy.

And now meditate on what happens to the Universe if God submits under the Law of Time and ends willingly.

But at least both agreed that God at that stage of development is not almighty anymore. He has to obey the laws of His creation Himself; He is victimized by His own creation. With His first step along the Ray of Creation, He lost His almightiness, or His almightiness is no more than His ability to either keep His creation going or destroy the whole thing, (which He will never do, because He admires His own work and loves AboraMana dearly, as we believe.)

But we also believe that the material universe one day sooner or later will dissolve against God's will, because that is the destroying effect of time and not even God can do anything against it.

In the spiritual universe something like time does not exist, because the spiritual universe does not have matter which appears to be solid when it comes in contact with other particles of matter, nor energy generated by matter, nor limited space, which are the three pre-requisites for the manifestation of time.

But in the material universe of humans on planet Earth, the one-directional flowing time is a solid reality, that's why the statement "time is an illusion" is so untrue and ignorant. Our life between now and the death of our material body—parted by time; our days between sunrise and sunset—parted by time; our moon-cycle, our music, they all prove that time is a reality; and understanding that clearly can teach us how to use time to our own advantage.

If you are in the unhappy position to give time a negative value, then you are fighting against overwhelming odds; you are a sure looser with absolutely no chance to win. So you better ask yourself the following questions and seek a truthful answer:

1. Why do I fear Sister Death? She is parted from me by time—she surely will come to meet me, but I don't know when.

2. Why do I entertain hopeless anger against grey hair, wrinkles in my face, and sagging breasts? This is an unavoidable time-process working on my material body.

3. Why am I forced to accept the time-values of the society I live in, and why do I accept being a victim of that force? Although I know that this position creates stress for my mental, emotional, and finally my material body.

Source: Vessel for Holy Water, used for cleansing rituals. Abora-Mana's cathedral in AtlantaCaldera. Giant Lapa-shell, diameter ca. 160 cm / 63 inches carved by an unknown master.

The carving shows the endless in one direction running time as a monster that eats itself without getting smaller or shorter, as it circles around the black hole of not-to-change-anymore.

This black hole shows you clearly that remorse about things past is pointless because of exactly that: It is not to change anymore, anyway.

Remorse is an emotional condition that follows a thing done wrong. It depresses you and hinders you to think analytically about what you did wrong; and that animates you to search for a therapist or savior who helps you to overcome your miserable emotional condition, which is pointless. And the use of legal or illegal drugs doesn't help either, it just worsens your condition.

What you need instead of remorse is (to make the following really work you better write it down):

The analytical definition of what you did wrong.

The analytical reasoning why what you did was wrong.

The analytical reasoning why you did wrong, connected with a search in your past whether this special wrong was the first wrong of this kind, or the last of a chain of the same wrongs.

Then honestly try to make amends for the wrong you did as much as it is possible in the present time.

The patient and humble bearing of the consequences of your wrong.

If you do that to the fullest, you'll probably never again do this same wrong—and only that is important.

The 3rd Plane of The Ray of Creation

Magic Physics

The Four Elemental Houses

The three sets of the Elemental Houses (the Gates, the Empresses, the Daughters) are closely interwoven, which makes repetition unavoidable. What is said about one card is valid—at least in part—for the other cards of the House, too.

Magic Physics / First Set

The Gates to the Houses

The Gates open the whole suit of their respective Houses throughout the deck; and all the cards of the House complement each other. That means when reading the cards and you draw a gate you should read all the cards of that House, too.

11 — The Gate of Air

Arts.
We don't need more artists, we need more inspired art.
Nature, spirituality, and art are one.

12 — The Gate of Fire

Family.
We don't need more sex, we need more Tantra.
We don't need more churches, we need better educated parents.
Also, never burn your fingers twice in the same flame.
Also, dramatizing a present time situation because of past similar experiences with a negative emotional loading.

13 – The Gate of Water

The Tribe.
We don't need more laws, we need better education.
Or, we don't need more police, we need more teachers.
Or, we don't need more prisons, we need better schools.

14 — The Gate of Stone

Traditions.
We don't need more knowledge, we need more understanding.
Also, on planet Earth, history teaches that history teaches nothing.
Also, holding on to traditions and old ways of thinking and doing things although they don't make sense anymore.

Source: These cards show the gates of the four cathedrals for AboraMana in AtlantaCaldera. The locks of the gates show the four holy animals of the Goddess in the four Elemental Houses; the bodies of the animals are shown as vertical symbols of infinity. The Gates of Air, Fire, and Stone are built on the model of the Gate of Water because the cathedral in the WaterQuarter is Her sanctuary since the first fishermen settled in the caldera.

Magic Physics / Second Set

The Empresses of the Houses

The Empresses are the Masters and
Teachers of Material Physics

They are the material elements like a storm, or a lava flow, or the ocean, or a pebble.

The Scientists of Magic claim that the Empresses rule the Elemental Beings of their respective Houses. The Empress of Water, for example, rules the Mermaids, they say.

15 — The Empress of Air

She can make herself visible to human eyes, then she is called an angel and she gives messages of warning of coming disasters of nature.

She loves to drive windmills and sailing ships and the big blue-water canoes. Gliders and parachutes are part of her responsibilities, too. Since she has less and less to do, she becomes restless and turns into tornadoes and violent storms, but generally she is helpful.

At her best, she is in the Trade Winds.

When she dances with her sister, the Empress of Water, they are called hurricane or cyclone, and they are beautiful, as we can see on satellite photos, and on photos taken from small sailing boats in a violent storm—or as you will remember when you sailed through the eye of the storm yourself.

As it is said in the port of AtlantaCaldera, a well-built and well-kept ship manned by a seaworthy crew has a fair chance to survive the eye of a hurricane. But we also know that there are freak waves out there no ship can survive.

Praise to Adam Eva's Son, the builder of ships, the sailor, the drawer of charts.

16 — The Empress of Fire

She rules the two worlds of fire—magma in the belly of Earth, and heat and light of the sun (but not the sun itself). She also rules the flashes of lightning between heaven and earth.

Humans also abuse her for the destruction of planet Earth, when they force her into nuclear fire or into explosives to kill other humans.

Some sects honor her as Sun-Goddess, but like her sisters she is not really a Goddess, but an elemental force beyond human predictions and control.

The Hawai'ian people honor her as Goddess of volcanoes, earthquakes, hot springs, and other seismic activities and call her Lady Pele. The scientists of Magic agreed on the name Lady Pele for the Empress of Fire to be used by the public because every scientist has to find his own, very personal name for her when he wishes to enter her House, and this name he has to be kept secret as not to loose his magic powers over the empress and the elemental beings of her House.

On the volcano islands, many stories are told how serious prayers can make Lady Pele merciful and that she redirects her lava runs to spare the fields and dwellings of the praying humans. One good example is the lava run of San Nicolas on the Canary island of La Palma where the HolyMotherWithChild helped the praying people, and Lady Pele saved the village, sending her lava flow north of the houses down into the ocean. That was in the year 1949.

17 — The Empress of Water

Her palace is the Pacific Ocean around the island Kiribati—also called Christmas Island—because this island is furthest away from all continental landmasses.

Triggered off by her sister, Lady Pele, she rises high and pushes her killer-waves far into the coastal plains and high up into the valleys, destroying everything on her way up, and on her way back, she drags everything with her and dumps on the ocean floor, for her Devis and Devas to play with. But she is also the one who makes those perfect waves every surfer looks and hopes for.

17 — The Mirror

The card of the Empress of Water you can turn around to see the mirror image. It is either a perfectly breaking wave, or the empress entering the hall in her most splendid regalia. That double face symbolizes water as the first and original mirror, and it serves as the symbol of the first question of a Human Awakening: "Who Am I?" which means, "Where is the mirror I can see me in?"

The cards Know ThySelf on the 8th Plane can be one of your mirrors to find out more about yourself.

The mirror also is often abused to serve human vanity—especially those of women.

18 – The Empress of Stone

Her throne is Ayer's Rock Uluru in Australia. Others claim it is the mountain Everest Tschomolungma in the Himalayas.

Every pebble, every diamond, all metals are her property. She is the one who despises humans most because of their need to comfort their vanity, and to fix the pecking order of a society who measures the value of a person on how many precious stones and gold pieces are in their treasure chests.

It was she who distilled oil and pressed coal out of AboraMana's children a long time ago.

At this stage no life exists on planet Earth, but the set is ready for the actors to play upon. The most impressive sets at this state of creation, like leftovers of the pre-life era on planet Earth, are:

The frozen continent of Antarctica for the House of Air.
The volcano Mauna Loa on Hawai'i-Island for the House of Fire.
The Pacific around Kiribati-Island for the House of Water.
Ayer's Rock Uluru in the center of Australia for the House of Stone.

A scholar of Magic Science, dedicated to the House of Stone, published the following paper:

Become aware of the difference between amulet (protector), talisman (enhancer), both called charms, and jewelry (display of vanity).

The "jewelry" of the pharaohs are actually elaborate amulets and talismans where each detail has a deep spiritual and magical loading, manifested as an electrical current humming through the body of the GodKing.

The best metals for amulets and talismans are Gold, Silver, Bronze, Copper, and the special one, Iron. According to the Laws of Magic, they are equally precious. Titan is good only for jewelry because its spiritual and magical properties are more on the dark side.

An amulet (protector) that came to you without you knowing how and that you wear always, be it throat or wrists, seldom changes, although there are minor amulets who protect only against one special threat, against the Evil Eye, for example. But you can have many talismans and wear one of them depending on what of your Inner Self you want to enhance.

Never wear a charm for vanity's sake.

Magic Physics / Third Set

The Daughters of the Houses

19 — Air – Visual Arts

The orchid and the butterfly (or the humming bird called colibri) symbolize the House of Air.

Freedom to follow spiritual goals. Following spiritual goals without love creates fanatics, missionaries, and religious wars.

Visual communication. Visual arts, drawing, painting, calligraphy.

First, where signs as means of communication with other members of the tribe about things of common interest. For example: An arrow scratched in the ground to show the direction the scout of the tribe went (down right).

Out of signs, symbols developed to show an idea or a concept connected to a SupremeBeing, the forces of nature, and religion (down left). A good example are the "spirals" of La Palma island. Nobody knows what they mean, but they are stone-carved prayers. The symbol on the card shows the double spiral as symbol for biological life and the sun wheel as the symbol for the spinning cosmos. (Tattoo design for the left shoulder of a girl.)

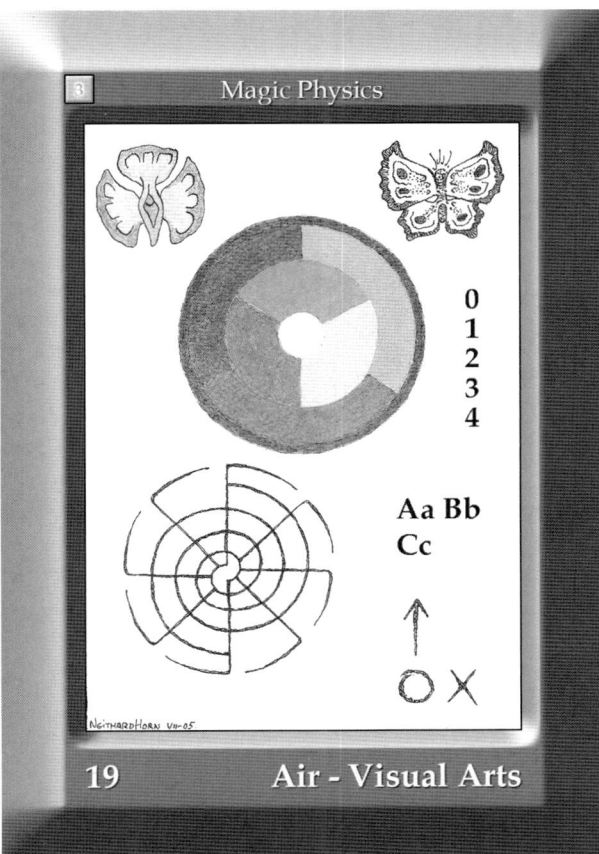

Out of signs also developed letters and numbers (middle right).

Then came the presentation of things that can be seen with the material eyes with first drawing and later painting, still connected to the religious life of the people, like the cave paintings of Altamira and Lascaux.

The orchid in the upper left corner of the card shows the artistic technique used for this deck of cards—watercolors washed over black outlines.

The circle of colors in the center of the card shows the three basic colors, their mixed colors, and the black and the white of the painting artist. It is the rainbow every aspiring visual artist should know because it is the theoretical basic of all working with colors.

Source: "On Visual Arts" by the author.

20 — Fire - Poetry

The Empress of Fire has two daughters, Heat and Light.

Chants, poetry, literature. With her sister, Music of the House of Water, she becomes songs.

Also, wisdom and knowledge destroyed; war, waste, torture; women, books, and art burned at the stake for religious reasons.

Also, propaganda, political lies, lopsided commercials.

Also, written history, on planet Earth mostly the history of wars written by the victors.

Freedom of speech. Speaking free without love creates arrogance in yourself and hurt feelings in others.

Discipline of Language: Know the exact meaning of the words you use, and use them free of emotional loading.

Mental discipline of language is the act of communicating a chain of thought in a logical fashion without big jumps, using the correct words to describe the thought, and the intent to follow the chain of thought of others while actively trying to understand (definition by LilithYggdrasil).

21 — Water – Music

The Empress of Water has four daughters—Spring, River, Lake, and the special one, Rain, all called Living Water, or Water of Life.
Music.
In an old Chinese book, music is described as the "mightiest of all arts" because music sends armies marching and helps soldiers forget their fear of death. Today, you may add: And can make 20,000 people dance in harmony.
Freedom to assemble. Assembling without love creates a chaotic mob or a mindless block of robots.

22 — Stone - Sculpture

Sculpture.

The freedom to wander and to live wherever you want. Understanding yourself as a free person on a free planet.

And the opposite: Borders, fences, walls, passport, visa, etc.

Nations, and the symbols of nations like flags and national hymns.

Patriotism, being territorial. Racism.

Source: Sculpture in the farmlands of Atlanta Island showing the matrilineal chain of generations. Ca. 2.75 m / 9 feet high. Colored concrete. Date of construction unknown, but old.

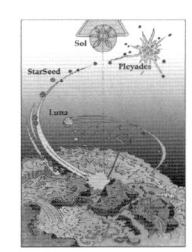

The 4th Plane of The Ray of Creation

The Science of Biology

Life and Death and AboraMana

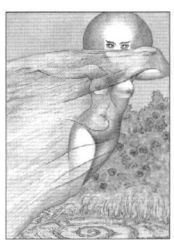

23 — Planet Earth Stage Two

If you ever have the chance to visit the biggest stone on planet Earth, Ayer's Rock Uluru in the center of Australia, the navel of the body of the planet, you will see a large chunk of the upturned crust of the planet, as it happened at stage two of the planet's history.

The rock is pure sand, pressed solid by the immense pressure of the layer of water over a zillion of years. Large pieces of the rock are eroded open, so you can look into the rock, but you won't find the smallest trace of life, like shells or ammonites, which means that the rock is older than life on planet Earth.

Sandstone is created by water dumping layer after layer of sand on top of each other until there is a thick plate of solidified sand on the bottom of the sea, as it was shown in the first stage of the planet's history. Because of the gravity of the planet, and the centrifugal forces of the spinning of the planet the layers are laid parallel to the surface of the planet, but in Uluru you'll find the layers rectangular to the surface. The rock is about 3 km / 1.86 miles long, measured along the layers, which means that the layer of sandstone must have been

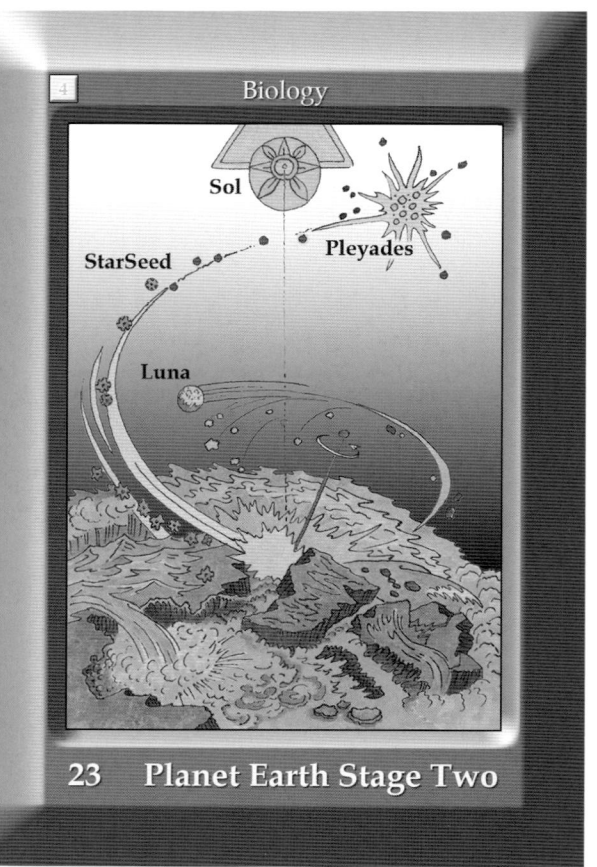

at least 3 km thick, probably thicker because the whole plain around the rock is the same sand as the rock, weathered off and blown away. And nobody knows how deep the rock is buried in the ground.

It is hard to imagine the force which entered the atmosphere, penetrated the layer of water, ripped out of the planet's crust a large chunk of solid matter, turned 90 degrees and slammed it back into the ground.

That must have happened, because otherwise the sandstone layers of sacred Uluru wouldn't lay—or stand—rectangular to the surface. Compared to that the destruction of Atlantis was a minor incident, that happened just sort of yesterday.

Some scientists claim that the chunk of interplanetary matter that hit Earth originates from the Pleiades, which was a prosperous planet until it was blown apart by it's inhabitants. They claim that with that chunk, Life rode to Earth as star seed, i.e., a single cell life-form that is able to hibernate indefinitely and survive outer space conditions. Naturally they can't explain *where* that star seed originates from before it reached the Pleiades and *who* created it.

But anyway, that chunk ripped out a large part of the planet's crust, mixed with it chemically because of the high energy-input and both-in-one continued into space, where they became the moon of planet Earth, which creates the eternal unrest of low and high tide in the oceans.

At the same time, the axis of the planet was knocked out of alignment with the sun, which creates the seasons of the Earth-year. And the impact made the planet wobble more around its axis as it was planned. And it turned the near perfect circle around the sun into an ellipse. And the magnetic field switched poles, which weakened it because of the residue magnetic energy in the solid matter of the planet caused by the former alignment. And because of the wobble of the planet, the magnetic north pole wanders all over the place, too.

It is also said that this breaking apart the stagnant harmony of Planet Earth, Stage One was a pre-requisite for biological life to come into being and to have a chance to survive and develop; which means that life can only exist in an off-balance harmony resulting in a constant unrest, varying from periods of relative calm to extremely chaotic circumstances.

Some scientists maintain that the changing of the tides, the changing of the seasons, and the changing of night and day are absolutely necessary for life on any planet, not only on Earth. That means, without the unrest of the Elemental Houses—exploding volcanoes, earthquakes, tsunamis, tornadoes, hurricanes, ice ages, draughts—without all the natural catastrophes on planet Earth, we and all living beings would not exist, so we better stop complaining about them.

And since we mentioned the moon: She changes with her phases also the weight of your body. In the nights of new moon you are heavier because sun and moon are situated under you and their gravities pull in the same direction. In the nights of the full moon you are lighter because the gravity of the moon above you neutralizes parts of the gravity of the sun under you.

And here is another thing: Color, and much more so the color of light, is an often underestimated energy. The silver-blue light of a clear full moon night (without electric-light-pollution) influences the feelings and behaviors of all living beings, especially of women. No wonder you feel so funny with the changing moon.

24 — Ur-Goddess Abora

The Primordial Goddess.
Procreating life without sex by dividing, and diversifying life by evolving and mutating.

At this stage of development, the Goddess is named by only the first part of Her name, Abora, (stressed on the first *A*), which means the Female Part of the Biological Creative Energy. UrGoddess Abora passes on life by dividing off parts of Herself without the help of any other energy but Her own while She transforms the matters of the universe of physics. And the most amazing thing is, She doesn't become smaller, but bigger and stronger in the process of dividing.

The divided-off parts are exactly like the ur-part they divided from, and they again divide into exactly the same form. The parts change by slowly adapting to a changing environment; or the competition for food and living space caused by other particles of Abora's body forces the life-form to adapt and thus develop and diversify.

The following explanation clarifies the concepts of *mutation* and *evolution* which are declared as being bull**** by some sects of

the dominant religion on planet Earth because nothing is written about it in their holy scriptures. Reason for this misunderstanding is inaccurate thinking about the Earth- or Material Body, the Mental Body, or the Mind including the Emotional Body, and the Soul or the Spiritual Body.

Mutation is a sudden jump in the genetic setup, and thus a sudden change of the appearance of material bodies in general, not only of humans, when the Energy of Life reacts to the influences of the universe of physics in an unforeseen and unpredictable way. On planet Earth, those jumps are mostly triggered by gigantic sun flares with their radioactive fallout. Many of the mutations—new life-forms that have little in common with the life-form they stem from—prove not fit for life, or not fit for the environment, and they die. Very few, maybe only one mutation out of many, are genetically stable and survive as a new life-form and pass on life by dividing and finding new niches in the environment in which to survive and procreate, as it is known of so-called primitive life-forms like bacteria and simple plants. And the same flare kills a lot of old life-forms to make room for the new ones.

Evolution is a slow adaptation of material bodies enforced by a slowly changing environment which in the very long run of time becomes genetically stable.

The bodies of today's humans and the bodies of today's apes are a stage of evolution in two different directions, after their common ancestor mutated into those two lines and then they developed to the present day forms. The basic difference between the bodies of the two lines is:

Less body hair but more head hair; the ability to stand up and walk on the hind legs as a normal way of life; a bigger butt to counterbalance head and shoulders. That leaves the hands with an opposable thumb free to fiddle around with things, and fiddling around with things creates inventions and new ideas.

The same mutation-jump, followed by two different evolution-lines also created new abilities of the analyzing mind of the new (human) life-form by an extended ability to learn. The more or less fixed commands of instinct gave room to the ability to reflect (analyze past experiences, not just react to them) and thus learn from past mistakes and successes; and to see into the future (if pretty limited) and thus learn to think in consequences, and with the enlarged knowledge came the human freedom of choice. The memory banks of the mind jumped and evolved from a few megabytes to uncountable gigabytes, and that created a consciousness of oneself as an unique individual, and thus an awareness of time, and life, and death.

After the jump, the mind developed by constant feedback from itself by use of memory and reflection, by constant updating the contents of the mind, and by the feedback from other members of the group of mutated beings. Thus the mind became a very flexible tool, interesting enough for a human Soul to manipulate and control her material body with. Only now, with a new body and a new mind, humans had the possibility to become the dominating life-form on planet Earth.

At this first stage of biological life, death happens only by being eaten by another life-form in a different state of development, or running out of food, or being killed by the forces of physics. Death by old age comes later with the creation of AboraMana.

In our understanding all biological beings thus created are XX, female, because they are the same as the source-being. That means that, at that time, the biological male energy XY did not yet exist.

And it means, XX is much older than XY, and it also means that XY is a mutation of XX. (The definition of *male* would be here: Sexually mutated offspring of a female source-being.)

To prove the point:

All the children of a fish called California Sheephead (Labridae Semicossyphus pulcher) off the California coast begin life as female, but some of them mutate to become male when they are 7 to 8 years old.

All the eggs of the crocodile are laid female (XX). Whether they turn XY (male) or stay XX (female) depends on the temperature of their place in the nest when they hatch. In the last consequence that means, Mama Crocodile is responsible for the sex of her children because she controls the place of the eggs in the nest.

On the Islands they tell the legend that for 90 years all the bamboo procreates by sexless dividing. Then they all bloom at the same time, some stems stay female, others mutate to being male. The females are fertilized by the males, and the males die. The females bear fruit and die. The fruit starts of a new female-only generation, procreating by dividing, till the next bloom. Whether this legend is scientifically correct, I do not know.

25 — AboraMana

The Split Goddess.
The Energy (Power) of Life.
The female sex-drive to conceive, carry, give birth, suckle, and take care of offspring.
The male sex-drive to ejaculate seed as often as possible.
She is also the source of all myths existing on planet Earth about women visited by gods to bear superhuman children.
The female sex-drive is the same through all animal life including humans (with comparably few exceptions); the male sex drive varies widely from strict monogamy (ejaculate in one female only through his whole life), or ejaculate-and-leave.

LilithYggdrasil / Lectures
About Egg and Sperm

(From the teachings in the WomanSchools)

In the minds of many members of the dominant society on planet Earth still spooks the legend how the sperms of the male have a race and fierce competition along the procreation canal of the woman to the egg ready to be fertilized. According to this legend the strongest sperm, which is there first, naturally wins and all others die.

Here we have the good old (male) story about competition, fight, victory, or death—the typical male thinking and acting applied to the process of fertilization. This legend reinforces the male domination of society and influences to the worse male thinking and acting on all levels of society (the strongest will win) and female thinking and acting (submit under the strongest).

But the truth is:

The sperms move up the procreation canal of the woman as fast as possible not to compete with each other but to get out of a slightly spermicidal environment, and the weaker sperms naturally die on the way up, which is AboraMana's, and thus the woman's way, of controlling the fitness of the next generation.

All surviving sperms attach themselves in regular distances to the outer skin of the egg, and the nucleus of the egg moves in spirals along the inside of the outer skin until she finds a sperm that she thinks will fit. There she softens the skin of the egg and allows this one sperm to enter and do his biological duty.

Therefore, the woman is fully responsible for the sex of the child and other genetic choices, within the limits of her sperm donor.

Yours truly, LilithYggdrasil
Teacher at the WomanSchool

There are rumors in town about how our girls in the WomanSchools learn to connect so closely to the egg, that she is able to mentally and emotionally influence the choice of the nucleus of her egg and thus influence the genetic heritage and the sex of her child. Whether that is true, I don't know, because the women are pretty secretive about their WomanSchools, and Gallia, when I asked her—naturally for scientific reasons only—with a sweet smile she refused to answer without clearly denying this possibility.

But all that at the side.

One of our legends tells: "She begged Her father for more life, for more love, until He split Her and blew His Odem into the split and thus He became Her lover and the father of all living beings…"

Another legend tells: "Abora grew strong and She sucked the spark of life out of God. To store the spark safely She opened Herself and put the spark into Her womb…"

And the two legends continue together: "…and through Her sacred portal came forth all animals. What does not come into being through the portal of the Goddess does not live."

From this moment on the Goddess correctly is called AboraMana because in Her the female and male energies of life are contained and since then all animals come as female and male. But to know: UrGoddess Abora and AboraMana exist beside each other.

God, the Male Creative Energy, starts at the highest level of mightiness and diminishes along His Ray of Creation until He is no more than the engine of that gigantic cosmic mobile to keep it changing, spinning, and in balance. He Himself has to obey the many laws of physics—which laws He needs to keep His creation going, and that naturally infringes His mightiness.

The Goddess of Life started very small but grows constantly bigger and stronger along Her Ray of Creation, because She has only one simple law: Grow! Diversify! Become more! (The academic definition of Life is something that becomes infinitely more unless it is stopped by Death.)

AboraMana occupies every nook and cranny of the universe of physics; She breaks down and utilizes every material matter for Her own growth; She adapts to God's energies of sun and moon, wind and rain, day and night most efficiently—in short, out of God's dead EnergySpaceMatter in the run of Time, She creates Life, and only She knows how, and no human will ever figure out what Life is. So don't even try, but stand back with respect and give a Prayer of Thanx.

Source: Illumination in a very old manuscript I found in our central library. The original is as big as the card you hold in your hands. Gold and colors of unknown origin on vellum.

26 – Life

That which organizes the materials of the universe of physics so that they stick together in the form of your body, for example; and that energy that makes your body tick that you can run around and sing and dance and emit a beautiful fragrance.

The materials of your body are solid matter, liquids and gases. They are called physical matter; they are understood as being static.

Life is an energy of unknown source that changes static physical matters into organic matters, which are understood as being flexible because of their ability to grow (become more), and decay, (fall apart) and turn back into static physical matters in a relatively short time.

One legend tells that space, matter, and energy in the run of time organized from simple to complex and gathered ever more energetic power during the organizing process and that at a certain moment of development the organized matter created life out of itself.

This card also opens questions about manipulating life-forms by cloning and genetic altering.

Source: Left part of a double page together with the following card 27 – Death in a book about biology.

27 – Death

Death cannot be known, only experienced.

This card shows the natural death at the end of the process of aging of the material body. It doesn't mean the so-called unnatural death by disease, accident, murder, or such like.

When the Energy of Life leaves a body that it doesn't tick anymore we call it death. She is AboraMana's beautiful but unloved sister, connected to her by an unbreakable umbilical cord. Between those two sisters we live, and it is prudent to learn to love sister Death, because the awareness of Her enhances human life and gives it deeper meaning.

One legend tells that God was forced to create death to counterbalance AboraMana's drive for ever-growing, ever-evolving life. Another legend tells that AboraMana *is* death, just as She *is* life—that She came into being as Life/Death. This idea is expressed in our Credo: "AboraMana comes and goes as She wills." That She is called Goddess of Life and not Goddess of Death is because life has to be there first before death can happen, and because we are, generally speaking, more interested in life than in death.

"I will die" is actually a wrong expression. Either it is the concept of: When my body dies, I disappear too, or it is used for easy conversation not to differentiate between I the soul, my mind (including emotions), and my body, all three together called The Holy Trinity.

Fear-of-death is the perverted Earth-body program AvoidPain, i.e., AvoidDeath which is part of the program DriveForSurvival. (Pain is death on a small scale—the cut in your finger hurts because some cells were killed by the knife.)

Fear-of-death works in the mental-emotional space of the victim and influences his behavior to the worse. The virus was put there by an educational process about matters spiritual. It took hold easily because awareness of death has the deepest meaning for every human, because death is unavoidable and unpredictable.

Awareness of death is short wired to the religion-matrix, which, when activated, is filled with what the parent generation thinks and feels about death.

In the dominant society on planet Earth, fear is put into the mental room of the victim by convincing him that he will be judged by a God after the death of his body, and that this God will deal punishment or reward according to the victim's obeisance and submission under laws he can't understand and can't follow because they are contradictory to human intelligence. Fear is created by "knowing" (but not being able to prove) that the punishment is cruel and eternal, with no appeal.

The dominant religion deleted the knowledge of reincarnation and rebirth in an Earth-body by sheer brutal force out of the consciousness of the humans under their influence. During the council of Nicaea, AD 325, the dominant males of this religion obliterated every text mentioning reincarnation from their "Holy Scriptures" and replaced with the righteously rewarding or punishing Hebrew male God. That move took away the god-given human right of free decision. From now on, the exclusively male caste of priests told the humans what to do or what not to do and claimed to speak "In The Name Of God," and they used fear, torture, and ritual murder to mentally and spiritually suppress the people under their influence. And again, don't be mistaken. They truly believed what they preached because they were just as well indoctrinated with the help of fear.

According to the legends of this religion, reward or punishment are doled out after one lifetime and the sentence is valid for all eternity without mercy. Either eternal bliss in the presence of this god, or eternal pain somewhere far away in the pit of a hell, depending on how far the human obeyed or disobeyed the laws given by this god as interpreted by his (male) priests.

Since the conclusion of the council in Constantinopel, AD 533, the propagation of the idea of reincarnation and rebirth was a spiritual crime to be punished by torture and ritual murder; and thus fear replaced the rational knowledge of reincarnation in the consciousness of the humans of the dominating society of the planet.

The dominating religion of the eastern culture kept the idea of rebirth, but their priests invented a Law of Karma, which again is a promise of reward or punishment, in this case not doled out by a god but by an anonymous karmic law. Karma is no more than the consequence of your thoughts, words, and acts. And karma, or consequences, exists only in the material universe, but not in the spiritual universe. There is nothing like good or bad Karma, there is only bad Karma because good Karma is the natural state of humans.

In the spiritual universe, also called InBetweenWorld, the Soul is totally free of sin and guilt. There the Soul is what she really is—a hologram of the SupremeBeing with a clear view on her past life filtered through her knowledge of good and evil. There the Soul decides if she voluntarily wants to go back to Earth to repeat her missed lections and wrong answered questions, and continue her lessons and experiences. And she alone decides whether she missed a lesson or gave the wrong answer to a question of human life, nobody in the whole cosmos does it for her.

In both societies, western and eastern, humans made life so miserable for other humans by war, suppression, and exploitation that a general despise of life on Earth (the Vale of Tears) and a longing for a perfect after-world (Paradise, Heaven) developed. And therefore humans forgot that Earth has been given to them as a gift with the challenge and the duty to turn the wilderness into a garden where all life-forms can live in peace and abundance.

Because natural death at the end of the natural process of the aging of the material body came into existence with the creation of AboraMana, i.e., with the dividing of life-forms in female and male, and with this division the procreation of life through sex, it was easy for the (celibate) male priests of the dominant religion in the west to connect sex and death and claim that sex is the cause of death. And because death was short-wired to the fear of a final judgment day, and because sex the cause of death, and because Eve, besides biting into the infamous apple, also invented sex and sort of deluded innocent old Adam that sex is something nice and necessary, the celibate male priests declared woman a second-rate human who needed to be dominated by men that they behave at least a little bit rational. And that is one of the many true reasons for the foolish behavior of men and women, especially in the spheres of erotic and sex in the dominating societies on planet Earth.

Source: Right part of a double page together with the above card 26 – Life in a book about biology.

Here I'm supposed to add some notes about our burial rites:

We bury our bodies in earth, or sink them in the ocean, naked as we entered this world through our mother's sacred portal, with no shroud and no coffin, adorned with flowers and green leaves.

Since our bodies live from the bodies and from the Energy of Life of AboraMana's children, the plants and the animals, we never burn our dead bodies. We know that during our life we are at the top of the food chain and to balance things out we consciously place our dead bodies at the very beginning of the food chain.

To avoid confusion: Nutrition-wise there is a big difference in that heap of ashes left over when you burn your body and that chunk of bio-mass that slowly rots and gets eaten away when you bury your body. Worms and plants do not need ashes to eat to go on living but they need bio-mass. Try it yourself. Burn all your food and eat the ashes and see how long you'll last; and do not make the mistake to see a difference between your own material body and the body of a worm or a rose.

And by the way, it saves a lot of stupid wasted fuel.

Yours truly, LilithYggdrasil,
Teacher in the WomanSchool

The 5th Plane of The Ray of Creation

Magic Biology

Plants and Animals / Devi and Deva

Devi are focused and crystallized Energy of Life as the "soul" of a plant; and a Deva is the "soul" of an animal. Every plant has a Devi and every animal has a Deva.

In AboraMana's system the souls of all plants are perceived as female and the souls of all animals are perceived as male, even when the soul lives in a female animal. However, our iconography permits the use of female forms to depict a male Deva—don't ask me why?

In the layout of the cards we lay the Devi before the Deva because in AboraMana's magic universe plants were created first and later animals; and because in the science of biology the female principle is older than the male principle.

It is necessary to state the fact that Devi and Deva are not Elemental Beings, like Mermaids for example. They are much younger because the Elemental Beings exist since the creation of SpaceMatterEnergy.

Because Devi and Deva love each other, they interact with each other. Many Devi use Deva for their sexual activities, for their procreation. Another reason is that the flowers are the sexual organs of the plants and they are often formed like the female sexual organ.

Orchids and peas for example, and many tropical flowers.

28 — Queen of Devi

The Queen of Devi is the symbol for all plant life on planet Earth.

She represents AboraMana in the universe of plants.

Devi (or Deva) are finite. She de-crystallizes and ends with the withering and the death of the plant she possessed and returns to AboraMana as a part of the Energy of Life.

The bodies of Devi and Deva resemble closely the bodies of humans, although they appear to each human observer different. They are small or big, depending on the life-form they possess and their body-forms and -movements characterize the Elemental House and the plant they stem from.

This card means TLC, Tender Loving Care, for all plants, not only your own.

Today be a tree hugger. Hug them really and tell them with spoken words how beautiful and strong they are, no matter how hard your friends laugh.

Source: Cover of the book of biology-lessons of plant life for our public schools.

29 — King of Deva
Male Fertility

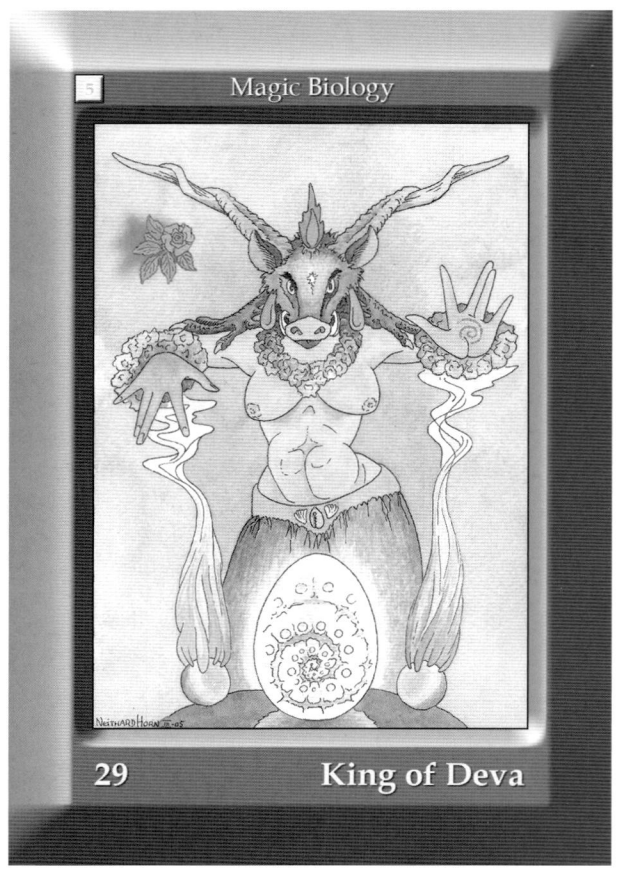

The king came into being for all animal life when AboraMana was split and all animals came forth out of her sacred portal. With each newborn animal, the Goddess creates a new Deva. They are very personal and they form the character of the animal.

The scientists of magic biology claim that the more you enjoy and praise and communicate with a special Devi or Deva the more they personalize and become real to you. They grow more happy and vigorous and give their vigor and happiness back to you.

The card shows the dance of a shamana to insure fertilization of farm animals. She dances around the mythological egg. The spiral in the egg shows the female Energy of Life, which is sleeping until it is awakened by the male Spark of Life, shown as the flaming balls to the left and the right of the egg. It is two balls because one carries the female sex and the other the male sex and nobody knows which carries which. Some scientists of theology claim that the male sperm carries not only one of the two sexes, but besides the Spark of Life also the Spark of Death.

Her hands hold AboraMana's mudra, on the palms are painted the female spiral (opening with the sun) and the male spiral (opening against the sun.) Her headdress shows our most important farm animals for food: the chicken, the goat, and the boar.

Masters of the science of Magic teach that every human with conscious knowledge and the appropriate training is able to enter one or the other of the Four Houses and communicate not only with the Elemental Beings but also with the Devis and the Devas of the House.

Source: Drawn during a shamanic ritual by the author.

The set of cards "Devi and Deva" refers to the erotic-sexual game played with a man; and later, when we come to the question: Who Are You? Define Yourself! You can use the Devi and Deva to help you to define your sexuality, which is the main purpose and function of your material body.

30 – Devi of Orchyd
House of Air

The young girl, the virgin.
Sexual self-satisfaction, and the hormone-induced female sex drive.
The exposed female sexual organ and the ability of woman to talk about it and to show it. (See card 55 – The Bitch.)
It also means, without shame, which comes from feeling guilty.
Shame has nothing in common with the natural shyness of a young girl.
Sehnsucht in German, which is a deep emotional condition of longing love for no particular reason and no goal or target.
In our iconography, flowers symbolize arts as nourishment of the emotional body. The orchid stands for the visual arts, because she is the "most useless but most beloved" flower in our world. She does not feed bees, or butterflies, or humming birds. She does not emit a pleasing fragrance like a rose or a sandal wood tree. She does not produce fruit to eat. She lives off the leftovers of other plants and gives nothing in exchange except pure beauty.

Source: A label of a flask of holy oil that is sold in the Mother's Temple on the island of Gea. I adapted that label to create a tattoo-design for the left shoulder of a girl.

31 — Deva of Colibri
House of Air

Erotic-sexual fantasy.
Erotic literature and images, perverted into pornography.
Transcending the sex drive into works of art.
To play the game of erotic and sex in daydreams and talk about it.
Tantra can teach you that, but recommends that in your daydreams you keep your fantasy on the erotic-sexual aspect and to be the actors only yourself and your man. It says, do not exchange your man for a prince-of-fogs and don't change yourself to someone you are not.

In some of our scriptures, the Deva of Colibri is replaced by the Deva of Butterfly, and here is a lecture about perfumes and artificial fragrances:

Butterflies and other insects orient themselves by smell. Smell is molecules floating in the air like colored balloons. The molecules of

smell are floating signs in the universe of butterflies, like the traffic signs in the universe of modern human transportation systems. They need those signs to find their food in the flowers by traveling along the molecules of smell of the flower (follow the yellow balloons), and they need them to find each other for mating by means of the molecules of smell of their potential mate (follow the red balloons).

Now imagine what you do to the universe of butterflies when you splash an artificial fragrance (mostly residues of the petro-chemical industry) on your body, be it shampoo, or soap, or perfume. You pollute their universe in an extremely heavy way. They can't find food anymore because the molecules of smell of your artificial fragrance like a snow storm block out the signs that are meant to help the butterflies to find food, and those she needs to find a mate.

Here you should find out how many molecules of smell are in one drop of designer perfume you apply behind your ear and how many molecules of smell a butterfly needs to find her way. I should say, block all the traffic signs and traffic lights of all major cities including air ports at the same time and imagine what will happen. And than you will know and hopefully understand what happens to the world of our butterflies with that one little drop.

Apart from that, what makes humans think that their bodies stink? And there are so many beautiful smells in the world of plants humans could use to adorn their bodies with.

I overheard LilithYggdrasil when once she was sorely pissed about human behavior. "I don't really care whether humans on Earth kill themselves, as long they don't kill the butterflies at the same time."

32 – Devi of Papaya
House of Fire

Passive sex.
Enjoy being used by your man without having anything to do or to go for; giving your body as a vessel for the pleasure of your man.
The "rape-game" including mild bondage if you both like it.
Also, the sweet smile and lingerie to seduce your man (see here card 72 – The Veil of Maya).

33 — Deva of Rooster
House of Fire

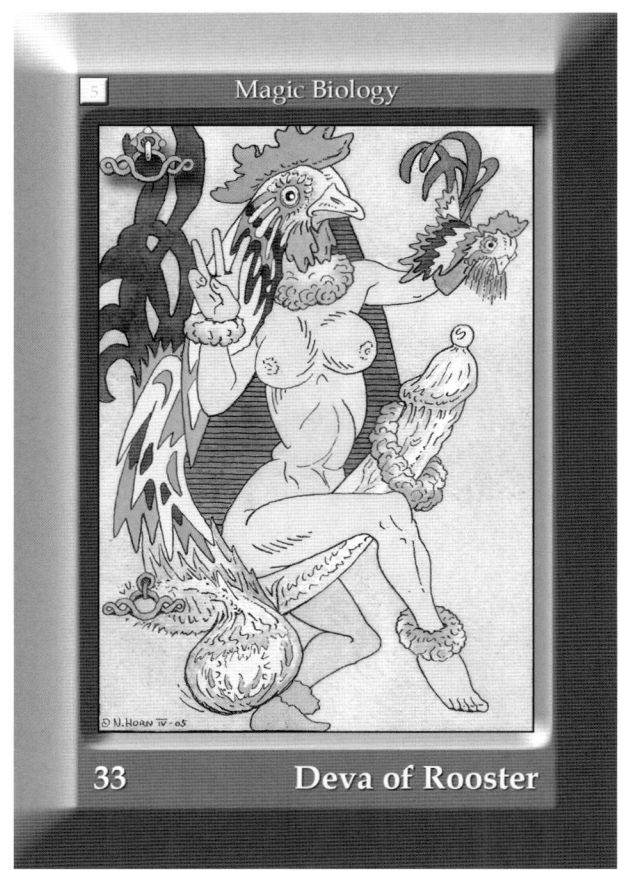

    Also, Three of Cocks. It stands for male sex.
    It is the genetically implanted drive of the male body to disseminate his genes as far as possible. That means to ejaculate as often as possible in as many different women as possible. This is a natural force that can't be changed. In some men this force is stronger than in others because of a higher testosterone-level, but every male has that drive. It is his AboraMana, the Energy of his Biological Life.
    For the good of the society as we have it right now, it is prudent for men (and women) to learn how to control that drive with the discipline of Tantra by using their emotional and analytical body to train the biological body what to do and how to react. This turns the power of the biological urge into a power of the emotional body, which reflects on mental body by deeper insights, and creates a feeling of highest well being in the material body. The problem at this moment is that you on Earth don't have enough women who teach Tantra. See here also card 41 – Tantra on the 6th Plane Human Kind.

    Source: This card I found in a small plaza in my hometown. It seems to be a card of a very old deck. Probably a child lost it while gambling. The card shows a costume-design for the annual procession in honor of AboraMana.

34 – Devi of Coral
House of Water

Aggressive sex.

Enjoy dominating the erotic-sexual game with your man.

Also, the Tantra-teacher who helps men to transform their sex-drive into an emotional power for the good of self and society.

In our understanding, the coral is a plant, because she misses our most important distinction between plants and animals. She does not move to new places to live. (See the Text to the "Queen of Devi," because much of what is said there refers to the "Devi of Coral.")

Corals are beautiful and poisonous—and even a simple scratch from a dead coral rock festers and has difficulties healing.

They are also sensitive to their biosphere. They survive only within small margins of temperature, amount of salt in the water, and depth. And they need the air in the bubbles of the foaming surf along the reef break.

Now just imagine what would happen if all the calcium and all the poison fixed in the reefs of the tropical oceans would dissolve and again become part of the ocean's waters, as it was before corals came into existence and started to build those gigantic reefs. Obviously, the beautiful corals are no more than a gigantic cleaning bio-machine that filters, holds back, and transforms in water dissolved chemicals. The ocean water as we know it today is actually the primordial soup cleaned up by the corals. The soup was much richer in calcium and less salty because salt was washed down from the land in an immeasurable long process.

Save our reefs!

Source: A good description of a Devi you'll find in the works of Clark Ashton-Smith, where he describes in one of his short high-density novels a group of Devi of Corals as "FlowerWomen," but places them on land.

35 — Deva of Cowrie
House of Water

Active submissive sex.
Enjoy finding out what your man wants and give it to him in abundance.
The classical courtesan.

Source: Around the tropical pacific rim, the cowry is seen as the sacred symbol for the genital split of the woman. In some places the cowry was used as a token of obligation and misunderstood by white man as money.

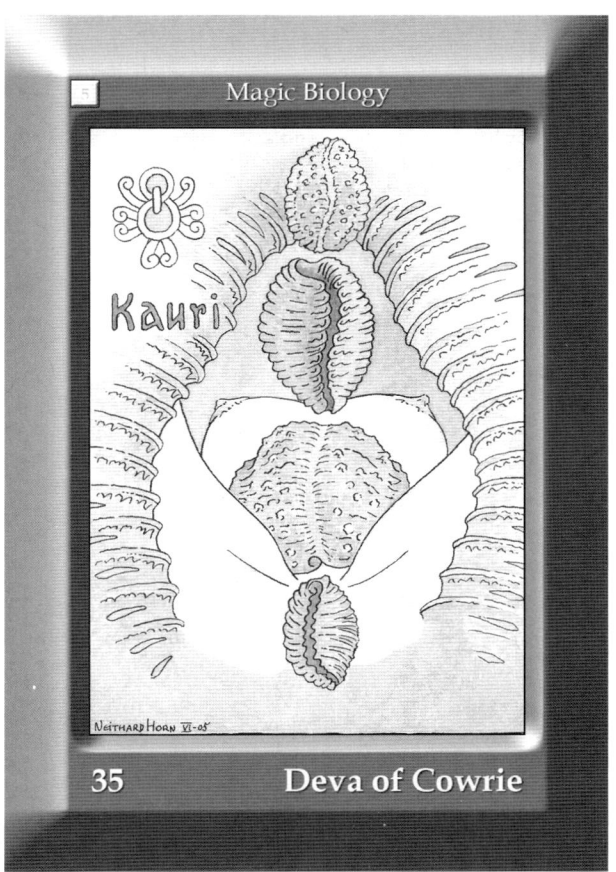

36 — Devi of Oak
House of Stone

Active self-centered sex.
Enjoy yourself and control your man to please only you.
Also, talking open about your wishes and desires.

37 – Deva of Lizard
House of Stone

Voluntary celibacy in contrast to celibacy for religious or moral reasons.

Not caring about the wishes and feelings of the other, which generally is considered a male weakness.

Being judgmental about the sexual preferences of others.

Considering the material body and sex as something lowly and dirty.

Rape, confusing pain and sexual pleasure.

Source: Mo'o is a Lizard-Goddess who lives on the south shore of Kaua'i and molests fishermen. Haagedis is of the Dutch language and means lizard. A lizard-girl that plays a major role in one of our educational children's books is called *Haagedis*.

By the way, all our children books are educational; that means—according to LilithYggdrasil—that they are always a notch higher than the child can grasp "to take advantage of the inborn curiosity of the little ones and make them grow by their own efforts to understand."

And since erotic and sex are closely connected to children, I'm supposed to give you the following paper:

LilithYggdrasil / Lectures
About Abortion

We consider abortion a problem that belongs into the hands of women, but not into the hands of men; and We will support every law that gives the right of free decision back to the individual woman concerned, without any interference by men.

Abortion is not a concern of the state and its laws.

Neither is it a concern of morals, which change according to social preferences, mostly for illogical reasons.

Neither is it a concern of a religion, no matter of what belief-system, or under which name this religion honors the SupremeBeing.

It becomes a moral, thus public, thus legal problem only, when one of the many one-and-only-true religions (mostly run by men) use the state (mostly run by men) and its laws to meddle in the private affairs of women.

Abortion is the physical, emotional, and spiritual problem of the individual woman concerned—and nobody else's.

The body of the woman is entirely her own, and only she has the right to speak and decide for it. Thus it is her decision to end the growing life within her or not. It might be the concern of the man who dropped his seed into her, but it can never be his decision because he does not own the body of the woman, and he does not own his seed anymore.

The emotions of the woman are entirely her own, and she alone has to face them and live through them her whole long life; and only women who have had an abortion can possibly understand her. No man will ever come close to understand the emotions of a woman in her condition, no matter how clear his memories of a former life as a woman might be.

Her spiritual life is entirely her own, and nobody is entitled to interfere with it. She alone has to face what she considers her SupremeBeing to justify her decision, and nobody is entitled to terrorize her by substituting her SupremeBeing with a judgmental god of a private belief-system to force the male point of view about abortion on the woman.

Yours truly, LilithYggdrasil
Benevolent Dictator

The 6th Plane of the Ray of Creation

Human Kind

FirstWoman and FirstMan

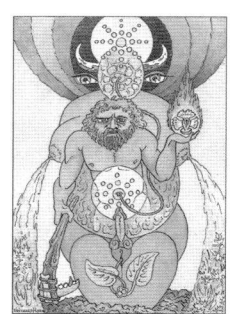

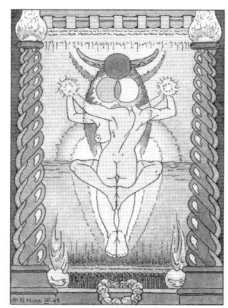

38 — Ur-Mother Eva

> Breathe in and breathe out.
> Drink and piss.
> Eat and shit.
> Procreate.
> That's all there is to a biological body.
> All the rest is just games and dramas you are playing.
> (From the teachings of the WomanSchool.)

The Mythological First Woman.

Havva: Hebrew = Woman, Mother, also: The Living, with the extended meaning, The Beautiful.

In the scriptures of the dominant religion on planet Earth she is called Eve, or Eva, and nobody remembers the origin and the meaning of the name anymore.

Our legend tells:

"The Goddess took red and black and ochre soil out of Her father's treasure chest, and formed FirstWoman's body into the beauty as we still see today, and She filled the dead loam with Her Breath, called AboraMana. And Her youngest child FirstWoman lived.

"And the Goddess brought Her living baby to the Devi and Deva, and they loved FirstWoman, their youngest sibling, and they called her Havva. The Devi gave her emotions, and taught her to see beauty, and the Deva taught her to sing and to dance, and how to make love.

"And the Goddess brought Her living and smiling baby to the Empresses of the Four Houses. They showed Havva the powers of physics and showed her God spinning the cosmic wheel, and they gave her the ability to ask, and to think, and to understand.

"And the Goddess brought the living, and smiling, and asking baby to Her Father. And God blessed FirstWoman Havva, His first human child, and He gave her the mental space, and filled the space with matrixes. He cross-wired the matrixes and timed them that they will be activated in their appropriate time. And then He kissed Havva FirstWoman and that kiss is You, You the Eternal Soul."

FirstWomen's body was given the form and the energy of life by the Goddess, given emotions and sense of beauty by the plants; given sounds, and movements, and ways to procreate by the animals; given the thinking mind by the Masters of Physics; and given the awareness of being the Holy Spirit by God.

According to the legends of the dominant religion on planet Earth, a male god created first a male human and later from a bone of the sleeping man this god formed the first woman, all this without MotherGoddess, which reflects the society who dreamt up these legends. It also explains, at least in parts, the unhealthy relationship of men and women in the dominant societies on planet Earth.

(Footnote to my Authorities: Sorry to say, the men and women in those societies don't realize anymore that their relationship is unhealthy. They see their attitudes towards the other gender as normal and unchangeable because they honestly believe it as a god-given truth that it *must* be that way.)

The legends of this religion also teach that the first woman—against the male god's will and without knowledge of the first man—took the forbidden apple from an evil being in form of a serpent, and then she tempted the man to bite into the sour apple, too, and thus she made herself guilty of creating an original sin, and, according to the dogma of the mother church—copied by all her sects—she polluted every human being without exception, from now to eternity, as if her sin was genetically implanted in all human kind and with no way to erase.

And that way the dominant religion condemned the First-Woman of their legends—and with her every single woman in the past, in the present, and in all future as long as the species homo sapiens exists—as being responsible for the miserable condition human kind is in, although it is a historic fact that the dominant males of human kind, including the high priest of the mother church, by war, exploitation, and oppression destroyed the fabric of human society.

And the men of the dominating society on planet Earth basically hate women, although they need them as a life-support-system for the pussy they need so badly, because they were taught that the devious woman led poor old innocent Adam astray, so it is her own fault that he lives in misery.

And here is one more thing: The dominant religion also gives the responsibility for the death of human bodies to the woman as punishment for the original sin, and to make things still worse, they connected with a grand gesture sex (woman) and death.

But the males on planet Earth couldn't quite hide the truth. Havva, the first woman, ate the apple of knowledge of good and evil and free decision. Havva, the woman, rose first out of the animal mind into the human mind by becoming aware of her own body's death and death all around her. She was the first who became aware of herself as an infinite soul, a member of the spiritual universe. And later she taught Adam knowledge and wisdom, and she made him socially acceptable by teaching him the difference between good and evil.

It is a simple fact that Havva by accepting the symbolic apple as the first human rose out of the sub-human mind of an animal to become a true human, because:

She realized that her body one day will die, as her God had promised: When you eat this fruit you'll die.

She realized that there is good or evil in human behavior, as Lilith the Serpent had promised her.

She realized that she was endowed with the freedom of decision because she was free to take the apple or not.

She realized that she was a hologram of the SupremeBeing, as Lilith the Serpent had promised her: You'll be like God.

And FirstMan Adam became a true human later than the woman and only with the help of the woman because Havva was so generous to share her knowledge and realizations with him.

And finally, Havva knew exactly that her body one day will die when she takes the apple, but she had enough courage to face that; to her the search for knowledge and enlightenment—the sign of a true human—were more important than her fear of her body's death.

The card shows AboraMana as the Eternal Goddess as the sign for infinity of the serpent-part of her body suggests. This part has a pattern in form of the double-helix of the DNA of biological life. She is also shown as the Horned Goddess of Fertility and Abundance, and as the Goddess of the Black Moon as symbol for the mysterious Energy of Life.

She parts Havva off Her body to show that woman is close to the Goddess, and they look similar to show that they are mother and daughter.

The Goddess rises Havva's head to show her the spiritual universe, that Havva will not forget that she is a spiritual being, that she will not forget who she is and where she comes from, and that life is more than just the material universe, shown as a spiral at the bottom of the card.

Source: Unknown

39 — Eva's Dream

Eva/Eve in her first stage of creativity called dolphins and whales into being by dividing them off herself, "and forming them with her hands, as her Mother had taught her. But the dolphins left her and went into the ocean and Havva followed them and she played with her firstborn children, but she was bound to the land by the will of her Mother," as the legend tells.

Maybe that is the reason why most people love dolphins and whales.

Source: Design for a mural.

40 — Adam Eva's Son

The Mythological First Man.

Also called, Eva's Reality, in contrast to Eva's Dream.

And then the legend tells: "When Havva returned to the land, she felt lonely and she cried to her Father for more life, for more love until He split her as He had split her Mother and He blew His Odem into her split, and as the time had come through her holy portal came Adam, a man, naked and helpless," as our scriptures teach.

Then the legend continues: "As Adam grew strong, Havva awakened the Spark of Life in him and taught him the sacred art of Tantra, as she had learned from AboraMana's children, and thus Havva was pregnant again and she became the mother of all humankind and her first son, Adam, became the father of all humankind."

According to the dominant belief-system on planet Earth, Havva was created for the sole purpose to satisfy Adam's sexual needs and to become the mother of his sons, Cain and Abel, and other children. Cain, the convicted murderer of his brother, Abel, is said to be the father of all humankind.

Some scholars claim that the legend of Cain and Abel shows the conflict between shepherds and gardeners, as society changed from a nomadic (Cain) to a agricultural (Abel) way of life. On planet Earth, the merits of women who invented and developed gardening and agriculture are not worth to be mentioned. But the true story is that the women kicked bad ass, when the goats and the sheep of the stupid males broke into their beautifully tended gardens.

Adam is a word of the Sumeric language that found its way into the Hebrew language. It means, Man Of The Earth, or farmer, gardener, and not Man Made From Earth. The idea that humankind is made from earth comes from the awareness that people sustain their biological bodies by products of the earth.

LilithYggdrasil's Lament

He is the genial maker of tools, but he uses his tools as a weapon against himself. In the process of killing himself, he also kills women, children, and large parts of life.

He is the daring scientist and he uses his science not to serve but to dominate life. In the process of dominating life, he kills life because life can't be dominated.

He is the tireless explorer and whatever he explores he conquers and subdues, leaving behind piles of garbage and dead beings.

He forgets that he is the son of a woman and the grandson of AboraMana and that he cannot live without them. He forgets that he is the servant of woman and AboraMana, not Her master.

He looks with pride at Stonehenge and he forgets that he built it as an expression of womanly wisdom, with women's knowledge, and under women's command, and every woman admits that he did a great job.

He knows that art is inspired by Higher Powers and is created to enlighten the world, but then he is satisfied with dead paint on dead canvas showing no more than the obvious.

He is a strong one and a proud one and every time his bloated ego feels belittled he turns violent. He is driven by his sex, by his foolish pride to be special and unique, combined with the animalistic urge to be the alpha-male in his field.

And worst of all, he is a genial inventor of justifications for his destructive behavior and the saddest thing is: He believes it himself.

And You, Woman!

Every time you do not control his search for the unknown, and every time you permit him to do as he pleases, he turns into the most destructive energy existing on planet Earth.

And every time you submit under his destructive energy, or more so when you encourage him by wanting more of his toys for yourself, you help him to destroy the very base of life for your children, and your own existence.

The card shows Adam in red as the color of earth to show that he was meant to be a "man of the earth," a gardener. Red is also fire as the color of the male energy. He is surrounded by the green color of life AboraMana. The Goddess is also shown behind him as the Horned Goddess of the Black Moon. She is surrounded by the rainbow colors of the night as the symbol for the female spiritual energy.

Through his umbilical cord he is connected to the mythical egg of life; the cord runs around his back to show that he tends to forget that.

The two blue circles with the stars inside are the Venus star as the symbol for the woman, and they are the symbol of the female Abora and the male Mana who have to be connected by the sexual act that new life can come out of the sacred portal of the Mother, shown as the first two leaves of a sprouting plant.

The Venus star of the mother has three circles on each of the eight rays, the Adam's Venus star has only two to show that he as the son of a woman is the secondary energy.

In his left (yang) hand he carries an orchid as the symbol for the female organ and the symbol for arts in general. The flame around the orchid means reverence for the woman, and art inspired by Higher Powers.

In his right (yin) hand he holds a tool to plough the earth that AboraMana the All-Nourishing can bring forth rich harvest, as it is shown in the milk of Her breasts. The red tooth in his tool shows that he uses his tools not only to plough but also to kill his fellow human beings and life in general.

This split mind is shown in the expression of Adam's face. He stares at you as if you would be his worst enemy.

He is Adam the torn one, eternally unsatisfied, constantly searching. But he just has to turn his head once and look at the Woman and the Goddess of Life behind him and realize that without them he is nothing and thus become the industrious, caring, honoring father.

Source: Unknown.

41 — Tantra

Tantra is the ritualized sexual intercourse of a woman and a man with consciously delayed and prolonged orgasm. One goal of Tantra is to feed the sexual energy into the emotional body and thus learn the unconditional love of God and Goddess. Insofar Tantra must be seen as a religious practice. Another goal is to keep your sexual energy—which is the pure Energy of Life, called AboraMana—inside your body for at least one hour. In that time the concentrated Energy of Life soaks into every cell of your material body resulting in a state of high well being. Tantra can be used as a therapy when you feel tired and listless.

According to our Scriptures, one of the most important first steps in Tantra is to learn honesty as opposed to shame, and clear verbal communication about erotic and sexual matters as opposed to only body-language, and the irrational demand "he should be sensitive enough to feel what I want."

LilithYggdrasil lectures: "Tantra is the only way to create in Havva's emotional body the dream state she was in when she swam with the dolphins. And Tantra is the only way to control and channel Adam's tremendous sex drive, which, when allowed to run loose unsatisfied, can be a very dangerous force out of Adam's control. That's why we invented Sacred Sex in the Temple.

"Our girls learn Tantra from the Madres of the Black Mantilla Sect, who refined the art of Tantra to the highest potential. The girl then teaches it in temple service when she feels like having sex with a man, until the day she binds herself to one man in marriage and thus becomes a woman.

"We have no girls and no young men with an unsatisfied sex drive running wild in our society. We have no prostitution, we have no violence against women or children."

And, I should add, we have no pornography, but a lot of beautiful erotic art.

The card shows two sandalwood columns as a left-turning female and right-turning male spiral forming this little side chapel in Abora-Mana's cathedral in the WaterQuarter of AtlantaCaldera. They are polished to a high sheen and they are crowned by two eternal flames. Below on the step of the altar are two balls with the flame symbol to show the female and the male part of the Tantra teachings. In between lies a garland with orange flowers dedicated to the Goddess as a Prayer of Thanx. This offer was given by a man because orange is the color of men (blue is for women).

On it's lower half the tapestry shows the world of water and of the woman from where we all come from; the top half shows the world of fire and the man. The heads of the couple are new moon for the woman (blue) and full moon for the man (yellow). The black superimposition of the two heads anticipates the Horned Goddess of the Black Moon behind them, shown as the third, black circle with the blue horns and the egg shaped black figure. Through the practice of Tantra the heads of the couple will merge more and more, and become the color of the Night Goddess in Her image, as it is shown by the shadows of the horns.

The hands of the couple are fireballs like suns to show that they don't hold onto something outside of Tantra but focus alone on themselves and the other. And to fold the hands with the other is part of the Tantra ritual because then the auras can flow freely and they are charged to maximum.

Source: Gobelin in the niche of a side-altar in AboraMana's cathedral in the WaterQuarter of AtlantaCaldera. Wool, silk, and cotton, ca. 2.70 m / 9 feet by 1.50 m / 5 feet. Artist unknown, but contemporary. She does not admit it, but I suspect that the artist is Our Reigning LilithYggdrasil.

For Adam, Eva's Son, to listen to:

Every rapist and every child-molester will be castrated and made totally impotent by whatever chemical means.

Then he will be kept in custody and professionals will try to heal his mental disease until he is either healed or dead.

We consider him healed when he accepts his castration as consequence of his crime.

In Our present times, We consider it necessary to issue this Draconic Law to protect our women who are the life of our species, and to protect our children who are the future of our society.

Yours truly, LilithYggdrasil
Benevolent Dictator

42 — True Love

Wanting to be at the same time at the same place where your lover is.

The card shows on top the Diamond of Total Truth and the rainbow of the spiritual universe and you and your lover as souls, as part of the spiritual universe (the two things like UFOs).

The right side of the card is female, the left side is male, (contrary to the general designation) and there you see the walls people build to hide their inner life. On the male side it is aggression as defense, on the female side it is deception and make-believe.

To create true love both of you need to break down the walls and open yourself for each other totally. As long as there is still something hidden, your love can't be true because part of true love is total trust and total acceptance, and that is either instant (love on first sight) or it takes a long time to be developed and nourished.

The lovers grow out of the spiral of the material universe; the spiral of the snail shows life, the skull shows the death of all biological life-forms including your body and the body of your lover. Part of true love is sex for the love of sex, but the procreation of life as your biological duty has nothing to do with true love.

The entwined bodies of the lovers suggest the double helix of life and show that they come from the same source and are therefore equal. The body of the woman is green in the color of

life, or as the color of the passive principle; the man is red for fire and the active principle.

The heads of the lovers are replaced by half of Mars for the male, and half of Venus for the female, both compliment each other to one whole, but they don't mix. That means that you don't even try to understand each other because no man can fully understand a woman and no woman can fully understand a man, and accepting that is part of true love.

Above it are the symbols and colors of the two sexes. The square around the circle is male, the circle around the square is female. This also symbolizes the emotional bodies of you and your lover. In true love they change their form and become one, but they can be taken apart without destroying one or the other. This shows that even when you become one flesh, you still are two individuals with each your own life and responsibilities. The golden color in the center of the symbols depict the souls.

Above it is the book of rules you need when you want to play the game of love, and you both must play the game with the same set of rules if you want to create true love.

It doesn't really matter what kind of rules you follow, but they must be the same for both of you. The rules can be changed, but only if both of you agree on the change. The rays coming from the Diamond of Total Truth show that your set of rules is part of the Total Truth, too. But both of you read the rules from a different angle; where your rules intersect there is total agreement, shown in the word TRUE. And the more agreed-upon rules you have the more stable your true love becomes.

Source: Unknown.

Since humans became self-aware, they also became aware of each other, and thus they became aware of the sex, color of skin, hair, and eyes, the body form and appearance, and the age of the other. To this general perception they apply a certain filter, called: Possible Mate? (There are other filters humans use to keep their sensory input below overload.)

This awareness of self and others as sexual beings is called the SexMatrix—it is implanted in the mind and activated during puberty. In an individual, the SexMatrix is divided into three equal parts, being responsible for the material body, the mind, and the emotional body as part of the mind. They serve the soul, which has no matrixes on its own. Awareness and a set of values acquired in the past concerning the opposite sex is part of the mind. AboraMana, i.e., the Energy of Life, works on the material body—being horny without any outside stimulation is one of its effects. Wanting to be inside an aura that spins in the opposite direction than your's is straight-wired into your emotions. That is why lovers love to sleep with each other. During deep sleep, after satisfying sex, your aura is charged to maximum by the opposite spinning aura of your man. This explains the Tantra rule: When you sleep with each other, sleep naked under one blanket.

(Here I'm supposed to explain that when we say sleep we mean *sleep*, we don't mean *having sex*.)

Besides the SexMatrix there are other matrixes, and all of them are activated at their own time, and all matrixes are cross-wired. And—I repeat—they do that in service of the soul. Science found that every human, no matter at what time, owns all the matrixes in the same form, at the same place, there ain't no differences in color or creed. The difference is only: What do you program into the activated sex-matrix of your child?

At a certain stage of the development of the material body, the SexMatrix is charged with AboraMana-energy and kicks in, ready to be programmed by stimulants coming from outside of the individual; they are sort of force fed into the newly activated matrix which has nearly no defense against it. The contents of the stimulants determine the mating behavior and the general approach to the other sex in every individual.

That means, depending how you, as part of the group of parents or teachers, stimulate the kicked-in SexMatrix of the young generation—*that* much you help to determine how the next generation of women and men feel about their own sex. This determines how they behave towards the other sex, which determines their erotic-sexual future, including the ability to feel happy. And, nota bene, the SexMatrix is an important part of the matrix called SocialBehavior. Needless to say, if the SexMatrix is filled with the wrong sort of stimulants, the social behavior of the adolescent will also be wrong.

True Love is not an avalanche that comes down on you out of the blue and buries you as a helpless victim. That avalanche-phenomenon is called *falling in love* and it is a symptom of a sexually frustrated society. You fall in love to justify the satisfaction of your sex drive, and when it is satisfied you just as easy fall out of love again, and all your sorrow and tears about a lost love is no more than a hysteric fit, although it may appear different to you.

True Love is a decision you make. You decide to love, and you are actively determined to keep your love alive. The decision comes out of your analyzing mind. You can only decide on rational reasons when you are not sexually frustrated, and when you have a clear perception in detail of the mental pictures you carry around in your mind about what you find attractive about males, including their bodily appearance. In short, you need to know some of the simple basics about yourself and be honest enough to check the compatibility of the contents of your matrixes against those of your potential mate.

Falling in love because the guy is so rich and famous, which makes him so attractive, is a very old part of the female sex-matrix to insure fertilization by good male genes, to make sure the next generation is well taken care of, and is strong and good looking.

But that was valid once upon a time, like the territorial fights with no holds barred of the males. Today, your submission under that primitive part of your sex-matrix is obsolete, because you have already convinced the world that you can be a good single mother.

LilithYggdrasil's Lament

I'm sick and tired of hearing people whine because they can't find their soul mate, their one-and-only-love in this life on planet Earth. I'm sick of hearing them dream about their soul mate of another life, in another universe, on another planet—but certainly in a most desirable body form of a human on planet Earth—man or woman, it really doesn't matter—just listen to their stupid love stories and you'll know what I mean.

We as self-aware Souls are as old as the spiritual universe. Since the beginning we did voluntarily choose to live in bodies of woman or man on a zillion different planets. We have about one and a half zillion soul mates out there—other Souls in female or male human bodies we met and loved during our roughly about a zillion lifetimes. So what's all that yakking about?

Why don't you get busy educating and transcending yourself into the soul mate of your man, in this here life on planet Earth?

That is the only way to find your soul mate: By becoming and being a soul mate yourself.

Yours truly, LilithYggdrasil
HighPriestess in Service of AboraMana

Pure Love, Unconditional Love, is a spiritual concept of the same value as the Philosopher's Stone; but it doesn't work between humans on the surface of planet Earth, no matter what their love stories try to make you believe. You love your man because: And then follows a long ladder of justified reasons why you love him. For example:

He gives you all the emotional and social security you need.

He lays you every two hours the way you like it best.

He is a good and stable provider and surrounds you with a luxury you think you deserve.

He is a good and caring father of the kids.

He opens the door for you to the rich and the famous where you think you can be a star.

And so on and on.

And if you think you are the object of his Pure Love you are sadly mistaken. He loves you because:

You give him all the emotional security he needs.

He can lay you every two hours the way he likes best.

You don't molest him when he's out with his friends getting drunk, playing poker.

You're a good housewife.

And I'm sure you can continue this lists. In fact, you need to do it in detail if you want True Love. And mistake me not, the fulfillment of the needs of the other—not because it is required but because it comes natural to you—are the fundaments of what True Love is between two humans in their daily reality; that's why it's so important to know thyself and check the compatibility of the above started list with the list of your potential partner.

The 7th Plane of The Ray of Creation

The Temple

Religion and Ceremony

As the title suggests, here we talk about organized religion, about that part of religious activity that needs to be organized to be functional. We talk about that part of religion that consists of rituals and ceremonies in honor of a SupremeBeing, but we do not talk about the SupremeBeing Self as defined in the ZeroCard.

We also talk about that part of religion that is the source of spiritual arts, that serves the organized religion by building temples, painting, and sculpting altars and sacred instruments, composing music, and hymns, for example. We talk about it in this context because the creation of spiritual art is a truly religious activity, as we find it with the ancient Russian icon-painters. They were deeply believing monks who saw the painting of saints and other members of the spiritual universe as a service to their God.

Looking through the millennia at the different cultures of human groups, we find that the forms of the religious activities are pretty much the same. That means all humans have the same idea about how, when, and where rituals and ceremonies should be performed to honor the PowersGreaterThanUs.

Even the reason *Why* is the same. Because of a feeling of overwhelmed awe, humans become aware of themselves as being one infinitely small knot in an incomprehensible big and incomprehensible intricate interwoven net of physical and biological creation. This becoming aware is called The Awakening Of The Soul. So they start to ask: Since *I* did not create the net of creation, *who* did? and *why*?

Humans Awakening are awed by the power and fierceness Father Creator gave His creation, by the harmonies, balances, and tensions that hold the net together, by the shine of the jewels of the suns and planets and rocks and pebbles woven into it; they are overawed by the beauty Mother Creator gave Her creation in the endless circle of life, of flowers and fruit, butterflies, singing birds, and our Humpback Whales.

And again they ask: Since *I* did not create the Energy of Life and all the living beings, *who* did? and *why*? And since my body is a living being, too, that lives through the Energy of Life, where does this energy come from? How come it keeps going and going until I die? And what will happen then to me who is aware of herself?

These two sets of questions are part of the ReligionMatrix every human is endowed with. The ReligionMatrix is activated—more or less intense—in every individual human.

Some humans are filled with gratitude when facing the two sets of questions, others are filled with fear, depending on the stimulation that filled the ReligionMatrix.

Gratitude triggers off a feeling of obligation towards the SupremeBeing and the Creators, or ThePowersGreaterThanUs, and a feeling of responsibility towards creation.

Fear triggers off the feeling of having to fight creation, like nature is the worst enemy of human kind, and to cut it down into tiny pieces that are small enough to fit into the mental space of the fearful.

All religions express themselves by having some sort of an altar with an image (ranging from abstract symbol to hyper-realistic rendering of a human being) that represents God and/or Goddess and that serves as a point of focus for the mental and emotional energies of the participants.

We have scriptures and chants about Gods/Goddesses, explaining the world from a certain angle and influencing human's social behavior; we have traditions that reinforce the scriptures; we have paraphernalia that symbolize the values that God/Goddess represent; we have ceremonies performed by priests or priestesses in special robes and their helpers, like musicians and dancers, acting within a certain choreography; we find a clear defined space that is constructed and reserved for religious purposes only.

The timing of such religious activities is either bound to the lunar/solar calendar, or it is a day of remembrance for something significant that had happened some time ago, always part of the tradition and often part of the scriptures.

You can divide this deck of cards into two sets, when you draw the dividing line between Science and Magic. Where the answers of science end, there begins magic.

Science follows creation to the Big Bang, but when asked: *Who* made the Big Bang and *what* did bang big? Science is lost for an answer. Magic says *God* and a whole universe opens.

Science can take apart plants and animals to the smallest particle, but when asked: *What* is Life? they don't know. Magic says *AboraMana*, and Devi and Deva come to life.

Religion definitely belongs to the Universe of Magic where human imagination becomes a three-dimensional reality.

The Temple / First Set

The Wall

43 — The Gate of AboraMana

The Sacred Gate is the Fifth Gate into the Elemental World besides the Four Gates to the Houses of Air, Fire, Water, and Stone. AboraMana's Gate opens to the House of Devis and Devas, and to Her suit in the deck.

The three cards of "The Wall" refer to feminine sexuality.

LilithYggdrasil teaches:

"You are the guardian of your sacred gate. If you invite Adam, he may enter, if you defend, he has to stay out, no matter what he wants. And that means, you alone are responsible for who enters your gate at what time. And that again means, you alone are responsible for having a child or not, or for you to pick up a venereal disease or not. Never blame Adam, because he is too blinded by his sex-drive and his bloated ego as to be able to take responsibility in that respect. His only responsibility is to obey you as the Guardian of the Gate unconditionally.

"Your responsibilities as the Guardian are not a burden too heavy to be carried by you alone. It is the honor and the pride of a woman who understands herself as the granddaughter of the Goddess."

(I think the old crone exaggerates, but basically I have to agree with her, being a man myself.)

Source: The only gate into "The Mother's Temple" on Gea Island.

Who built that gate I couldn't find out, but it is of first class craftsmanship, built of the finest limestone I've ever seen and I've seen a lot. You can't fit a piece of paper into the seams between the stones. Considering the social setup on Gea, I suppose that men built it under the supervision of the Old Mothers, but I might be wrong and the Mothers built the gate themselves. The entrance is ca. 4 feet high, between 12 and 24 inches wide, and about 9 feet deep before it opens into the high central cupola with is illuminated only by a round sky-light in it's center, and a few candles along the circular wall, burning quietly. As far as could see in the blue light of the full moon, the dome is an artificially expanded and smoothed cave. In the center of it is a ca. 15-foot-wide platform, about 3 feet high, carrying the life-sized statue of a nude young woman. As I came closer and my eyes got used to the mellow blue light I saw the sculpture was not a sculpture at all but a very real and very alive girl who stood motionless on the platform to be admired by the visiting men.

Carved into the adjoining rock is a spiral connected to the tree of life. This is AboraMana's glyph in our 13-month zodiac, which, by the way, would make more sense on planet Earth, too. I painted the wall and the gate when I visited Gea on government mission and I really had a hard time to convince the Old Mothers (sort of priestess-rulers of this particular AboraMana sect) that I may take my drawings off island, and about my government mission they wouldn't give a ****. As grouchy as the Old Mothers were, later they were so friendly to sell me a flask of their holy oil, which they use during their unique Tantra-rituals. The label of that flask I used for the card "Devi of Orchid."

44 — Defense
45 — Invitation

Carved into the rocks again you'll see a spiral connected to the tree of life. The spiral is the female spiral, because it opens and becomes infinite *with* the path of the sun through the heavens. The male spiral opens *against* the sun, as the male instruments of watches and clocks also run against the sun.

Here I should add the legend, well known to humans on Earth, how women of an ancient Greek tribe by defending their Gate against their men prevented a war.

As I visited the Mother's Temple on government mission I noticed some men at the temple wall who carved female figures and abstract symbols into the rough stones like those shown on these cards. As I asked them whether they do this because they were ordered by the Mothers to do so, they just shook their heads and explained that the carvings are prayers to the Goddess and the Mother, and they were doing this "since the very beginning of all times."

Source: Petroglyphs on the dry rock wall of The Mother's Temple on the island of Gea., ca. 4.5 to 6 m / 15 to 20 feet high.

44   **Defense**

45   **Invitation**

The Temple / Second Set

The Main Altar

These three cards are replicas of the three panels of the main altar in honor of AboraMana in Her cathedral in the WaterQuarter of AtlantaCaldera.

As said before, AboraMana has a different name in the different Elemental Houses but I don't remember them all. I only remember what She stands for in the different Houses. As Lilit, AboraMana of the WaterHouse, She stands for intuitive emotional wisdom; in the House of Fire, She stands for uninhibited joy of life; in the House of Air, for free floating curiosity (other sources declare that here She stands for unlimited creativity); and in the House of Stone, for inner strength and peace of mind.

46 — Lilith AboraMana

The Horned Goddess.

The central panel of the altar shows Lilith AboraMana as the Horned Goddess, the gentle Goddess of Fertility and Abundance. The Indian holy cow has its source in this image. The horns also symbolize the crescent of the waning and waxing moon that embrace the Black Moon.

By the way, when you imagine the crescent of the moon as a bow with a notched arrow, the arrow always points straight into the sun.

She wears a sunfish because it is Her holy animal in the House of Water. The sunfish is an octopus that never stops growing, the perfect symbol for life. The same sunfish is shown in the great mosaic that decorates the Old Harbor Plaza of my hometown.

She grows out of the spiral of the material world of physics, She is decorated with the swirling dance of life. The netting of Her gown shows that She is part of the cosmic fabric, the seams are DNA-strings and the egg and the seed of the two sexes. Her jewels are green leaves and roses as the symbols for life and beauty. She is crowned with the

Diamond of Total Truth, which on Her points downward to suggest the down-pointing female triangle and to show that She the mirror image of the Total Truth. The frame shows the tree of life growing out of the female spiral. This is Her sign in our 13-month zodiac, as the Roman cipher for 13 indicates.

To know: AboraMana's zodiac has 13 moon-month, and each month has 4 weeks and each week has 7 days. The day starts at night when the first star is visible in the sky, and ends with sun down the next day. Among others, this is Hebrew and ancient German and very feminine.

Source: The Main Altar in Lilith AboraMana's cathedral in the WaterQuarter of AtlantaCaldera. Central panel of three, oil on wood, each panel approximately 180 cm x 120 cm / 6 feet x 4 feet, artist and time of creation unknown.

47 – Lilith Eternal Goddess

The Goddess of the Black Moon.
She stands for intuitive-emotional wisdom.
The dark nights between the moons are Her nights.
Hers is the thirteenth month in our zodiac, when winter is darkest.

As said before, in each of the Elemental Houses AboraMana has a different name and a different iconography, but She is always Goddess of Life, Love, and Beauty, Goddess of Fertility and Abundance, Our Mother without Navel. In the Elemental House of Water, the Goddess is called Lilith AboraMana, in short Lilith.

On planet Earth wet dreams of sexually frustrated men have falsified Lilith to be a beautiful woman's body (!) with a snake's end, dark wings, and totally evil intentions towards humankind, like blowjobbing—because she can't spread her legs—"unwilling" men and robbing children. She is the one who gave Eve the apple of knowledge and wisdom and thus doomed humankind to eternal, not erasable sin and damnation, as the dominant religion on planet Earth teaches.

The left panel of the main altar shows Lilith AboraMana as the Eternal Goddess. She wears the Diamond of Total Truth with the point up because She comes straight from The Source. The lower end of Her body—the snake—is formed like the endless double-loop that symbolizes eternity or infinity. She floats above the spiral that is the universe of physics to show that the universes of physics and biology are two different things. The open eyes on Her wings show that She never sleeps and that She is one-and-many at the same time.

The roses in her veil symbolize beauty and love and all plant life, the pearls and buds on the other side of her veil symbolize the joy of sex, and the egg and the seed of all animal life.

On this painting, the sunfish as Her holy animal in the House of Water is missing although in our iconography it is a must, and nobody knows why, in spite of that, the HighPriestess gave her permission to place this painting on the altar of her cathedral.

48 – Lilith Chaos Goddess

The Goddess of Disorder.

The moment the primordial soup exploded into life with infinite possibilities open.

Dark emotions triggered off by hormones and/or low air pressure.

"The Goddess of a Girls Purse." She reigns when you can't put an order in your material possessions, no matter how hard you try. But, as LilithYggdrasil teaches: "Give praise to the chaos-goddess and forget about order. Be happy in your chaos because it is the order you need right now."

On this painting, too, the sunfish is missing. Before the guild of artists and artisans declared the sunfish as an iconographic must, a picture of a snake was sufficient to symbolize the Goddess as the Goddess in the WaterHouse. Maybe the missing sunfish reflects the age of the artwork.

Possibly the following remark is of interest because it shows how our Reigning LilithYggdrasil runs the business of government.

She strictly refused her permission as the chemistry boys from the Research/Discovery-Center on the other side of the harbor offered to check out the age of the art work with the most sophisticated means available at present time. She reasoned: "What for? Except you, nobody is interested in that. And I do not want anyone of you running around in my cathedral waving stinking chemicals. And you can pray without knowing how old the paintings are."

In this context, another incident seems to be enlightening. As the scientist of the R/D-C wanted to sound the depths of the harbor (*guestimates* run from 300 m to 1000 m) she again refused her permission. "What is deeper than 50 m is not the world of humans anymore, and a little mystery is good for you because it teaches you respect. And I do not want you to disturb our holy sunfish down there."

The holy sunfish down there is allegedly a gigantic octopus living in the depths of the harbor pond. Nobody knows for sure, although some people claim they had seen it in full moon nights drifting just below the surface of the still waters. But to tell the truth, those people walked home over the Old Harbor Plaza after a long lasting visit in Carlito's "Fisherman's Sinkhole" under the LighthouseRock.

The Temple / Third Set

Prayers

Prayer is the communication between humans and the Creators of the world we live in, and with the members of the Spiritual Universe—generally called PowersGreaterThanYou, or the Host of Heaven. In organized religion, prayers adopt the style of chants and hymns to enable every participant to join unison and thus magnify the energy of the communication.

Architecture—the circle of stones of Stonehenge, the pyramids, the European Gothic cathedrals, for example, are non-verbal prayers; as are often music or paintings, basically all inspired arts, it depends on the form and who is addressed. Temple dance, on the islands called Hula, is another form of prayer.

In our prayers we never forget that we are equal to the members of the spiritual universe, and we don't forget that we became humans because we were the only ones in the whole spiritual universe who had the guts to experience the edges and hard knocks of the material world in a material body; we are here not because we are weak and stupid, or for karmic reasons, or as a punishment, but to feed our experiences in the material world back into the spiritual universe.

49 — Cleanse with Water

House of Water.

This is the proper place to admit that I'm not a friend of ceremonies and rituals because painting is prayer enough for me, and I consider ceremonies as a waste of time. But this my strictly personal point of view. I honor and respect all ceremonies, no matter what creed celebrates them. The more colorful and elaborate they are, the more I enjoy them as a great show without feeling a great urge to take part. Therefore, I can't say much about these cards. But if you find your own interpretation feel free to add to your personal script.

In my prayers, I never beg for something, I only give Thanx, not at a certain time or at a certain place, but always when the beauty of creation or the love of a true human looks straight into my eyes.

If I want something good happening to me in the future, I sit down on a quiet spot, as far away from human works and human noise as possible, and dream it up in my mind, three-dimensional lasting through time, in full color, and around that image I wrap all my emotions of final fulfillment. And I do that often for a long time.

Anyway, I drew these sketches during the Ceremony of Thanx for good harvest and good fishing in Lilith AboraMana's cathedral in the autumn before I left home, and I observed very well LilithYggdrasil's half frown-half smile as she observed me drawing.

50 — Cleanse with Fire

House of Fire.

Washing your hands in smoke to make them ritually clean before performing a ritual or a ceremony.

Cleansing a space with incense or sage to get rid of unwanted vibrations or unclean memories.

The frankincense of the Roman Catholic Church as an offering for their deity, and similar smoke offerings as part of religious practices.

And here is a prayer of an old American Native chief. I heard it a long time ago, and I forgot some of the lines, but the most important lines stuck in my memory:

>Oh great spirit
>Whose voice I hear in the wind
>Here I stand as one of your many children
>Hear me
>Make me wise that I understand the lessons you have written in every stone and leaf
>Make me strong to fight my worst enemy, my own laziness
>So when my time comes I can stand before you without shame

The so-called war-bonnet of the prairie tribes was actually prayer-bonnet to straighten out the face of the praying into the wind, which was their symbol for the SupremeBeing.

51 — Grace for the Flowers

House of Air.

Temple dancer presenting flowers to the audience who send all their Thanx into them. Then they are dedicated to the Goddess and placed on Her altar.

In our culture, flowers symbolize beauty, love, life, and arts. As the bread and the fish are the food for the material body, so the flowers (and the arts) are the food for the emotional body.

LilithYggdrasil teaches: "Be careful what you feed your emotional body with. If you feed it with emotions that do not root in love and beauty, you'll poison it, and then you'll get mentally sick, and that will destroy your material body."

52 – Thanx for our Food

House of Stone.

Temple dancer presenting bread, fish, and wine to the audience who send all their Thanx and gratitude into the food, which then is presented to the Goddess and placed on Her altar.

See also, The Lord's Prayer of the Christian faith, "Give us this day our daily bread;" with the explanation of Martin Luther (abridged and adapted): "What does it mean: Our daily bread? Everything that is necessary for body and life—good food, clean water, clean air, clothes, home, money, good spouse, good government, peace, health, true friends, good neighbors, and so on."

53 — Prayers Answered

House of AboraMana.

A Hawai'ian man called Roots told me the legend how the Goddess of Abundance riding on a blue turtle brought all the fruit and animals to the island of Kaua'i, and how the Humpback Whales sing the praise of the Goddess.

The descending Goddess brings our most important farm animals: the boar, the goat, and the chicken (see King of Deva) and all the plants we can use for food or just admire—three sprouting coconuts, taro plants with their triangular leaves, breadfruit, bananas, and much more.

The owl and the bats stand for the universe of animals outside of human use—why they are both animals of the night I don't know, maybe because you can't even keep them as pets. And there is a funny looking lizard sitting at Her feet.

She also represents the contents of the word ALOHA, which is a Prayer of Thanx for the abundance of flowers and food we live in, shown on the material plane as: "Share, enjoy, there is enough for everyone," and it is given free without expecting that something has to come back, because here is abundance anyway.

Source: Illustration to the legend, "How Abundance Came To Our Island." *The Book of Legends for Children.*
Kapa'a Beach, Kaua'i

The Temple / Fourth Set

The HighPriestess

54 — Our LovelyOne

House of Air.
The Kindled Fire.
Honor Your Children.
Self-love.
Queen of temple dancers.
Learn and teach dance.
    Drawn from memory after I left the island of Gea, because I couldn't take my draw tools into the Temple. Men may enter only naked as they where born, excepting their charms and amulets and their flower crowns, and garlands.
    The painting shows the central cupola of the Mother's Temple in a night of full moon, with a LovelyOne standing motionless on a platform in the middle of the hall to be admired by the visiting men. The Old Mothers (sort of priestess-rulers) told me, that a LovelyOne is a young girl in training of dance and martial arts to become a temple dancer, and that presenting herself in that form and standing motionless for hours is part of the training. She wears the temple dancer's

tattoo, which is given when she commits herself to the order of the temple dancers who are elite in the art. But the Gea-men truly believe that she is a lifeless sculpture carved by a master.

By the way, the men of tropical Gea live in villages in the coastal plains and the foot hills of the rugged island; the women live as priestesses and dancers in the temple city which is taboo for men. What the women do in their temple city is unknown; the men are good farmers, who give half of their produce to the temple "because it seems to be right to do so," as they explained when I interviewed them. They all are good musicians in a sort of gamelan-music for temple dance; the best groups travel with selected temple dancers throughout the Inner Islands on an annual schedule to play during the temple festivals. And they are the best sculptors in our world, if a little one-sided. They sculpt nude women only, depicting OurLovelyOne, their most beloved manifestation of the Goddess. Their work holds little miniatures of imported precious stones, and life sized figures of good stone or tropical hardwood which they plant and carefully tend; or big concrete sculptures which they build in team work; and everywhere in AtlantaCaldera on the stairways, the plazas, and galleries you find those beautiful Goddesses from the island of Gea.

Song For Adam to Listen to

Adore her and let her be as she is
Let her do as she does because she is doing her best
You are not her leader.

If something on her disagrees with you
Leave her but don't try to change her
You are not her teacher.

And if she wants to go let her go
Give Thanx to her and cherish the memory
You don't own her and you are not her jailer.

55 — The Bitch

House of Fire.
The Wild Fire.
Honor Your Spouse.
Self-discipline.
Learn and teach Tantra.
Sacred prostitution
—which is not prostitution because there is no money or anything else involved. It is part of the Tantra training. The Bitch teaches Tantra to the man who asks her as she has learned, or she refuses companionship. Within her self-discipline she is free.

Unmarried women and men meet at sundown on the Old Harbor Plaza on the stairs of AboraMana's cathedral. Men bring apple cider and snacks, women bring candles and flowers, and all bring their ukuleles, flutes, and drums; it is like a party.

Source: Illustration in our Tantra theory book, chapter one: Love yourself and love your body as it is. (Literally: "As the Goddess gave it to you.")

56 — The Mother

House of AboraMana.
Honor Your Parents.
Self-observation, self-restriction.
Learn and teach the traditions, the rituals, and ceremonies.

Part of this are the teachings about the movements and interactions of the celestial bodies, also called astronomy and astrology. Our WomanSchools are run by mothers.

Also, work in the sense of: To work for money is the lowest motivation; to work for the joy of it is next higher (but then it is not *work*); and the highest motivation is duty.

Never work, but always be busy with something constructive and creative.

The card shows the Great Mother in Her UrForm. She stands on a base of clay symbolizing the universe of physics. Her lei shows her womanhood with the five-cornered flowers, and her masculinity with the yellow circles, like the ball with the flame symbol and the flowers at her feet. On her left thigh she wears the tattoo of the order of the temple dancers.

Images like that in all sizes and all materials you find everywhere, in every temple or chapel. Kiddies have soft dolls in her form, and in art class it is the first figure to be formed in clay. Many artists of the stone age on planet Earth connected to that piece of art and copied it. The best known example is the Venus of Willendorf.

Source: Small altar piece in AboraMana's cathedral in AtlantaCaldera, imported from Gea Island. Translucent glass on a stand of clay inlaid with precious stones, ca. 112 cm / 45 inches high.

57 – LilithYggdrasil

House of Water.
Old Tree Roots In Earth And Carries Sky.
The Tamed Fire.
Honor The Old.
Being impartial, or not personally attached to someone or something.
Judge / decide / command.
Law and law enforcement.
Law and Right are not always the same; Right is always Law, Law is not always Right.
Self-education and teaching others.
Also, power, which is, get rid of your inhibitions.
Also, the tyranny of the mediocre.

LilithYggdrasil, short Lilit, ChairWoman of the GreatCouncil in her function as acting HighPriestess wears the hood of a shamana, symbolizing Lilith AboraMana, the Goddess of the BlackMoon in the Elemental House of Water. The BlackMoon symbolizes intuitive womanly wisdom—the snake whispering in Lilit's ear. The colors of the two flower garlands around her neck show that she is honored and loved by men and women alike. She reads the scriptures explaining the ZeroCard and teaches the technologies you need to find it. On her gown she wears the zodiac sign of the LilitMoon—the tree of life growing out of the female spiral—as the sign that she speaks with AboraMana's Voice.

She has seen and done it all, but she seldom talks about it. She was a temple dancer (I think she was trained on Gea), she trained and taught Tantra and the art of fighting, she worked in the Taro fields, and went out fishing, she bore and suckled children, so all her teachings are based on her own experiences. Among the other women of the GreatCouncil she was selected by the Old LilithYggdrasil to become her successor and she was trained by her and the members of the GreatCouncil to become a Lilit. She told me as she recruited me for this difficult mission on planet Earth that she objected strongly to carrying the burden of being a Lilit, but was overruled by her feelings of responsibility to our society.

She created artwork that is highly respected by all knowledgeable people; during her reign, the big mosaic of a sunfish was laid on the Old Harbor Plaza. It is said it was her design, selected among many other anonym submitted designs by the Guild of the Artists and Artisans. More than any other LilithYggdrasil, she married carefully chosen daughters of the City to the warlords and petty chiefs of the Barbars to strengthen the civilizing influence of AtlantaCaldera.

Source: A cartoon I drew of our Reigning LilithYggdrasil in full regalia during one of her lectures, to the great amusement of the whole population including the old lady herself.

When you cover half her face with another card you'll find that on one half she smiles and the other half she frowns. I have no idea how that happened when I sketched her in pencil. Naturally I exaggerated it as I drew the cleanup in black ink.

To avoid confusion:
LilithYggdrasil is not the name, but the title of the Chairwoman of the GreatCouncil, the HighPriestess in Service of AboraMana, and the Benevolent Dictator of the Empire of AtlantaCaldera.

The members of the GreatCouncil are all the women of the City and, when they are in town, every woman from the Inner or Outer Islands, too, even if they are Barbars and have no idea about our system of government which is

Anarchy for All, combined with the
Democracy of the GreatCouncil, and
Lilit's Benevolent Dictatorship.

Her Dictatorship consists of that in the end she decides and enforces what has been found in the democratic process of the GreatCouncil and in the general consent of Anarchy for All.

Anarchy means "without government, without ruler"; and according to my thesaurus it means "the absence of any *formal* system of government in a society" (stress on "formal" by me). It definitely does *not* mean throwing bombs and creating general havoc. And the synonyms my thesaurus offers are misunderstandings of the old Greek concept Anarchy, like chaos, lawlessness, revolution, disorder, or a situation in which there is a total lack of organization or control. All this is *not* anarchy, and it is about time to clear this misunderstanding. Only well-educated, honest people of good will can be anarchists.

An early LilithYggdrasil set the tone of government for centuries to follow. (But She refused her permission to carve the maxims in the rock face above the Hall of Justice with the reasoning: "What for? Either people know it, then they don't need a reminder; or they don't know it, so who cares? It just means that we govern our people right. And I like the rock face as it is; I sort of got used to it. And all that dust and noise in my cathedral…")

The best government is the one
people don't notice.

Well-educated people
don't need a government.

Humans are tolerant, cooperative,
and they love to share
when government doesn't exploit them,
and allows them to live in peace.

To know: The benevolent dictatorship of Lilith Yggdrasil is counterbalanced by the office of the Tribune as the speaker of men, who more often than not agree with Lilit's decisions. He was the one who knocked down every objection I had at being recruited for this difficult mission on planet Earth, instead speaking up for me against Lilit's demands.

58 — The Ancestors

House of Stone.
Ashes, dust.
Honor Your Ancestors, and the work they did for you.
The work you pass on into the future of your family, your tribe, the whole population on planet Earth.

Song for Havva to Listen to

Listen, my daughter.
Voices whisper out of deep past:

We once had the power and life was good for all
until we enslaved those serving us willingly
until they revolted—and look at us now.

Listen, my daughter.
Regain the power that rightly is yours
but don't make our mistake.

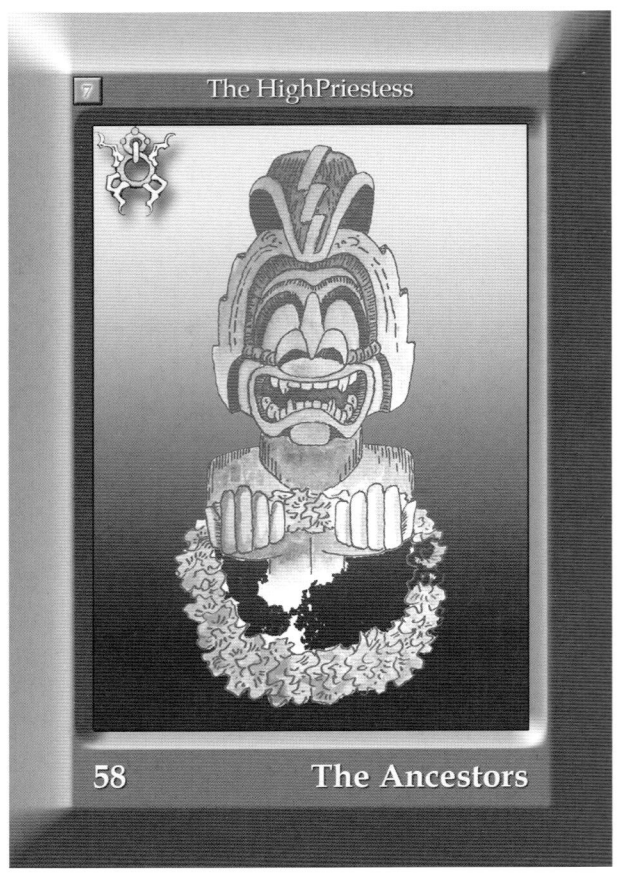

The Feminine Wheel of Life

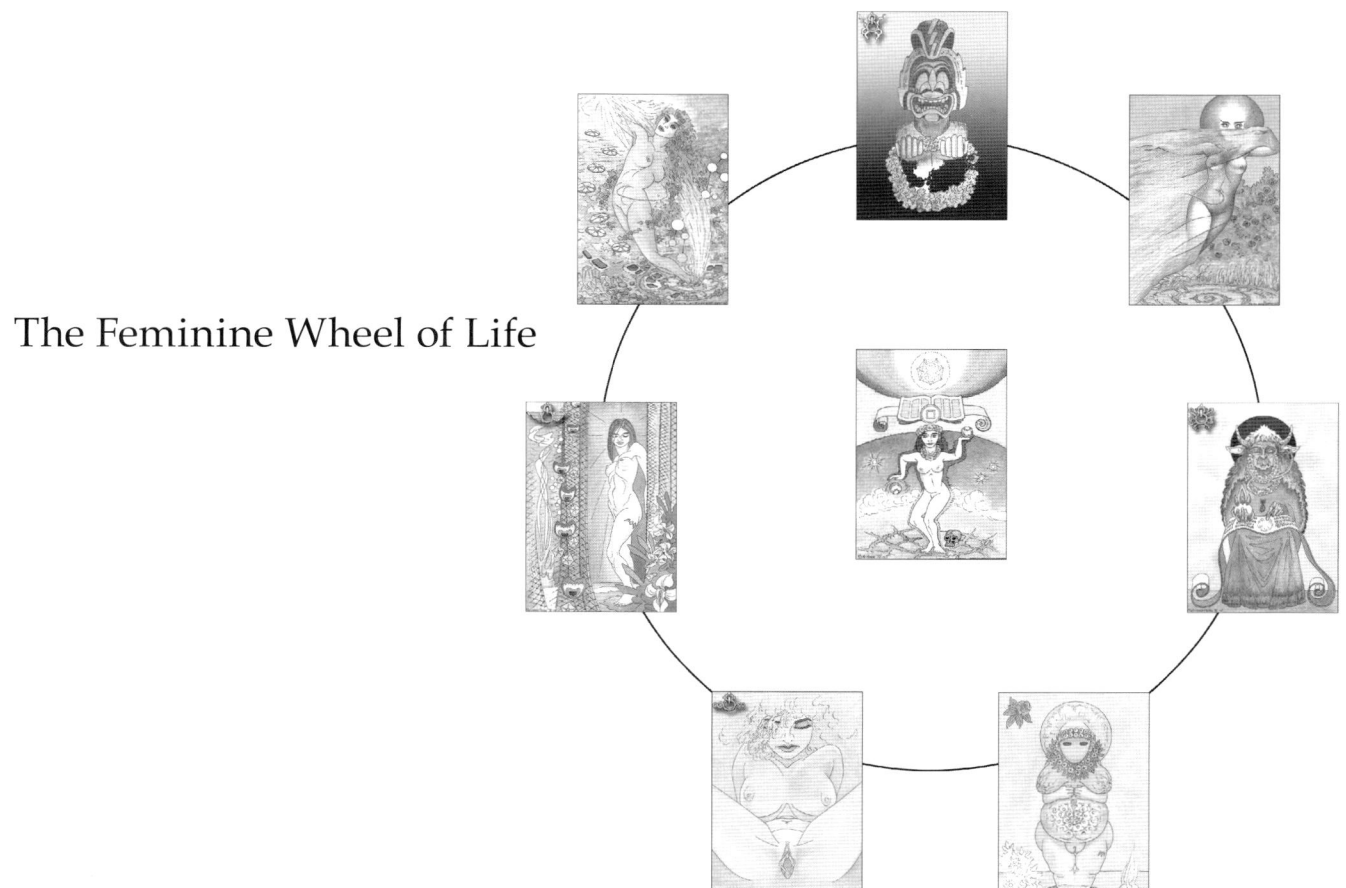

The life of woman proceeds in six distinct steps
connecting six distinct planes.

First step
Your birth
First plane
Your life as a child

Second step
Your first blood
Second plane
Your life as a virgin—Our LovelyOne

Third Step
Your first full sexual contact with a man
Third plane
Your life as a free woman—The Bitch

Fourth step
Pregnancy and giving birth
Fourth plane
Your life as a mother—The Mother

Fifth step
Your last blood
Fifth plane
Your life as elder and teacher—LilithYggdrasil

Sixth step
The death of your body
Sixth plane
You as a memory; the life of your children, and
your life's work that lives on—the Ancestors

The card Ancestors between the cards of Life and Death as part of the Wheel shows you that you will be reborn into a world that has been influenced—that means that it has been, in parts, created by you.

WomanSchool teachings say that you have to walk the path between the steps to the fullest, and when you have to take the next step forced by the powers of nature, you will take the life essence of the past path with you over the next step. And when you have to leave that path, you take along two sets of essences; and when you reach the step of your death, you will carry the five lives of the HighPriestess with you. The teachings say that this is your duty for being a woman and enjoying the privilege of having five lives.

The Wheel of Life is connected to the Spiral of Learning—the Wheel runs on its own, the Spiral is your very own responsibility and effort. With the conception of your body and your birth, the Wheel of Life begins turning and you start the process of learning; with your death, the wheel stops and you end your lessons on a higher plane. In the between-world, you pause to reflect about your past life, and to define the lessons you want to learn on the Spiral of your next life. There you also decide whether you want to be born as a woman or as a man, who will be your parents, into which culture you want to be born, and the time when you want to return to planet Earth. (All this according to the *Tibetan Book of Death*, and those Lamas know better than anybody else on the planet what's going on in life and death because they have the most advanced InnerSpaceTechnology— why do you think the Maoist Chinese, self-declared materialists, want to destroy their culture?)

Again and again: You alone decide. You are not forced by a PowerGreaterThanYou—they might help you to make up your mind, but you alone decide. There is no Karma. It might look to you like Karma, but it is not. You begin the lessons of your next life at exactly that point where you ended your lessons of your former life—be it higher on the spiral, or, if you wasted your life, be it lower—sort of repeating the class. The empty threat that you might come back as a cockroach when you were really bad is no more than that—an empty threat. The idea of good/bad is only a human prejudice, anyway, and it works only on the material plane and only in human societies. Humans come back as humans because only humans can learn.

Learning is possible only in the material universe. Learning is an additive process in a one-directional linear time, stacking one piece of information after the other in the appropriate compartments of your mental space and connecting them with each other. To learn, you must remember, and remembering again is connected to time because you look in present time at something you learned in your past.

Because there is no time in the spiritual universe, neither the Host of Heaven, nor YouTheSoul, as a member of the Host of Heaven, can learn because they live in an eternal present and are perfect, anyway. In this context, the definition of "human being" would be: A member of the spiritual universe who is willing to take the tight corners and difficult spots of the material universe in a material body to supply the other members of the spiritual universe with emotions about experiences while going through the school of hard knocks.

The Temple / Fifth Set

The TempleDancers

The dancers reinforce and enhance the prayers of the congregation, and their dance is considered as a Prayer of Thanx expressed with the whole body, like the old Hula of the Hawai'ian people.

---

59 — Dancer of Air — Lyrics

Self-love.
Self-love without love makes you greedy.
The more you love yourself, the more you will love everything else.
Live what you are, never stop learning to become what you can be.
Learning from others by observing and asking.
This is the first card I painted (June 2004 on La Palma Island) just for the joy of painting, not knowing that I had started a whole deck and not knowing that I would write this script.

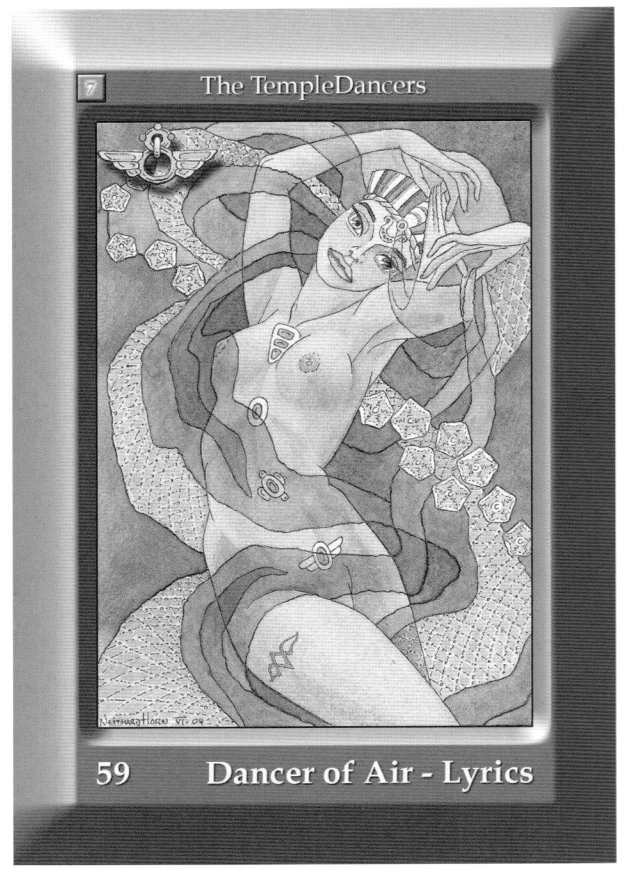

60 — Dancer of Fire — Drama

Learning by experience to find out your likes and dislikes, your abilities and limitations, your goals.

Learning by your own experiences, making your own mistakes. Nobody is entitled to judge whether you made a mistake or not. Every experience is one lection in the school of your life. Basically, you can't make mistakes because they are part of your process of learning. But if you make one experience again and again and keep feeling bad about it, than you're making a mistake, and that is what you could call committing a sin. But be assured, sooner or later you will learn this lection, too, like you learned all other lessons presented to you, otherwise you wouldn't be here right now.

Self-discipline: Forcing yourself to do something although your body and your mind protests, but it seems sensible and rational to YouTheSoul. This is the only way to change habits and become flexible again. Sometimes you need help from the outside.

Self-discipline without self-love makes you overly demanding of yourself and impatient towards others.

Exaggerated self-discipline can lead to self-destruction.

61 — Dancer of Water — Rhythm

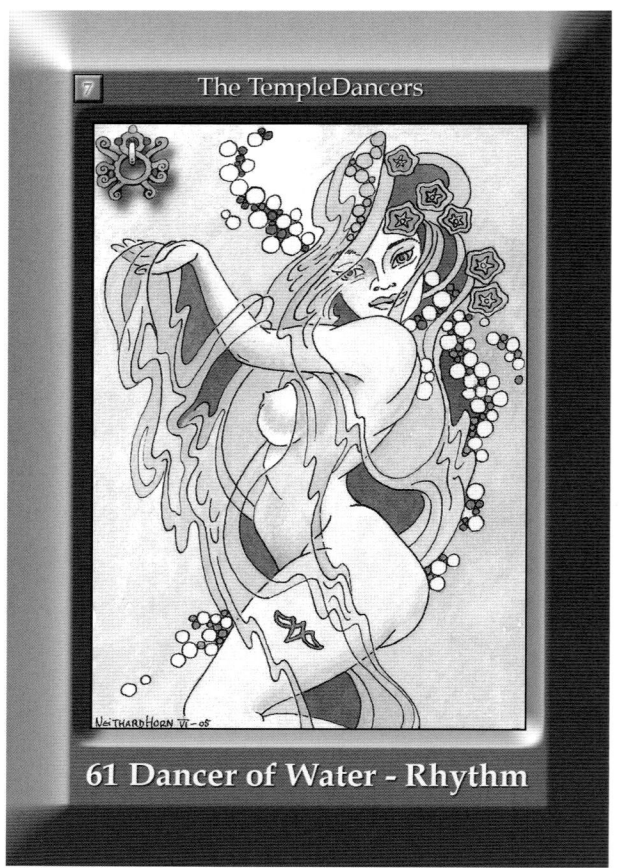

Self-control.

First step of self-control is self-observation. This is a mental ability and should be learned and trained. Start by observing your feelings while you are doing something; after some training you will be more and more able to see yourself from the outside. Then you have to apply self-steering to continue what you are doing, or stop doing it. That's all about self-control but it is absolutely necessary to find your own way through life.

Also, be your own slave driver.

When slave and slave driver cooperate, they generate joy and peace of mind; when they struggle against each other, they generate a torn mind, and in the long run a mental disease called schizophrenia. (Split brain, or split mind, but it is not the dual personality syndrome).

LilithYggdrasil, MindHealer

Self-control without love makes you uptight and hard towards others.

Also, self-control without self-love leads you to self-deception, which means that you think that when you control yourself hard enough, then you are able to reach a goal you are not cut out for. (In German this is called *Lebenslüge*.)

Learning by reflecting, which is evaluating the experience by observing your emotions about it to find out what the question of the lesson was, since already you have the answer.

62 — Dancer of Stone — Style

Self-education, Self-motivation.

Self-education without love makes you narrow minded and intolerant.

Learning for the joy of learning, for the joy of growing mentally.

Learning by teaching. Teaching makes you understand better what you know intuitively.

Learning by walking the Path and knowing the Goal.

The old saying "the Path is the Goal" actually means: To *find* your personal Path through life is your goal, which might not be as easy as it sounds. Free floating through the incidents and opportunities offered by life is not your Path. Doing what others tell you to do isn't your Path, either. Once you've found your Path, you just walk it and then there is no goal anymore except to walk your Path as fast and as far as you possibly can.

Before you came here you knew your Path, but you decided to forget it, because finding your Path again is part of your being a human on planet Earth. You will know that you found your Path when you see it is endless, filled with self-imposed problems and difficulties, which are the steps of your Path.

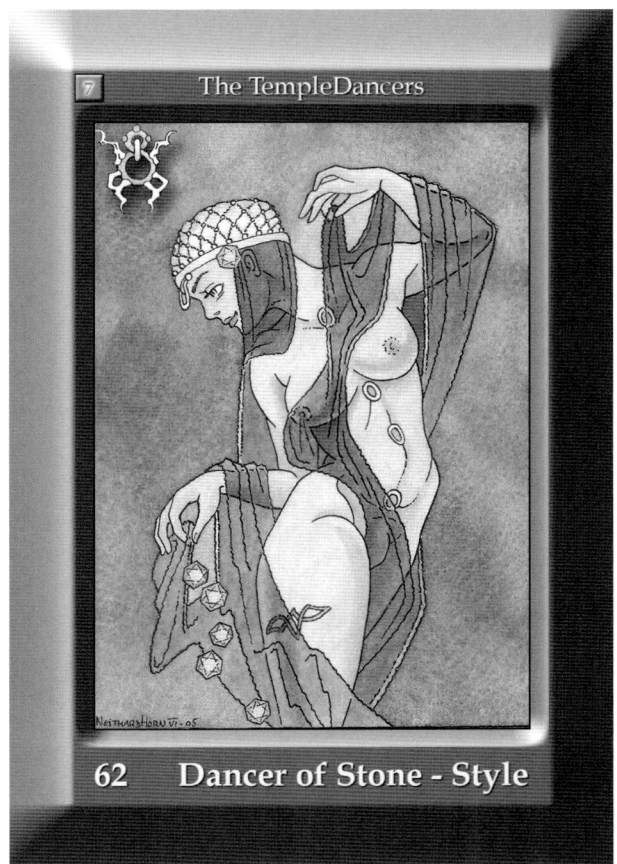

63 — Dancer for AboraMana

Original title: Our Mother Kaua'i.
Uninhibited joy of life, love and beauty.
Love in the spiritual, emotional, and physical sense.
Enjoying sex for the joy of sex.

She represents Life, Love, and Beauty, which do not need any interpretation or explanation, because every human has a powerful matrix connected to it. She also represents the contents of the Hawai'ian word ALOHA, which is Sharing as a Prayer of Thanx for the abundance of flowers and food we have been given by the powers of nature. Aloha has very little in common with what we call hospitality for strangers because of tradition, or necessity, or morals.

I painted her purely for the joy of it because I had nothing else to do: As a Prayer of Thanx for me as who I am and what I am able to do; being here where I live; doing what I am doing in perfect surroundings. And the self-imposed problem and difficulty was to give her the Polynesian color of skin. While painting her, I did not know that she would be a very important card of the deck; at that time I seriously thought the deck was finished.

She is so young and beautiful because every child sees Mother as the MostBeautiful and I see me as Her child, and I know She loves me.

The five golden flowers point to the parts of what you are—they are not chakren and they do not suggest an order of importance or value. The lowest flower, the orchid, is your female earth-body, the flower above is your emotional body. The sunflower in the middle are all your activated or not activated matrixes, as a part of your mental body. Then comes that part of your mental body that is your analytical understanding, and finally that part of you that is self-aware, all of them having their male-parts. The white flowers behind her right ear tells everyone in the language of flowers that she is looking for a true lover.

The 8th Plane of the Ray of Creation

You

The Holy Trinity

Goddess loves you
you are one of Her most beautiful children
you are the center of Her universe
Her whole world revolves around you

you are the little girl
you are the lover
you are the mother
you are the wise old woman
you are the creator of the future

all this is you—and more
no matter what you think of yourself

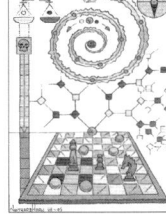

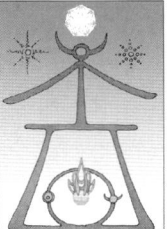

64 – This is You

On top of the card you find the Diamond of Total Truth to show you that you are a part of the Total Truth—the hologram of the SupremeBeing, created by a God or a Goddess of your choice. You are one facet of the Diamond, and everyone of your fellow humans, including Hitler and J. S. Bach, is another facet; and every other spiritual, mental, and material phenomenon, including Hiroshima and 9/11, is another facet.

The Diamond is surrounded by the empty space of creation, and by the rainbow of the spiritual universe. You are aware of yourself as an individual spiritual being and you know that you are eternal. This is the real You, the Soul. Part of You is to be curious and to love to play games, and that brought you here. You came here on your own free will, not as a reward, not as a punishment, not for so called Karmic reasons, but because you *wanted* to be here as a woman for the greater glory of Goddess and God, and you came here to show the universe the most beautiful expression of Their love for each other.

The rule of the game you agreed upon before you came here is: When you live in a human body on planet Earth you will forget that you are You, a Soul. You will also forget your past. That is the back-to-zero or open-new-game effect. Goal of the game is to see the Total Truth, which is no more than to remember who you are. But this is something you forgot, too. To trigger off the search you become aware of the death of your material body and the big question: And what happens then? The hidden knowledge that you are a part of the Diamond and the imprinted, not yet activated matrix of the Hall of God make you a magnet for esoteric, spiritual, and/or religious experiences, which activate certain parts of your ReligionMatrix, which trigger off new questions about yourself, which the Diamond and the activated matrix will answer by telling you who You are. Since the Total Truth is endless and since the matrix the Hall of God as the first level under the Source is nearly endless too, the questions and answers will grow bigger in their scope and more interesting, but they will never end, and that is part of the fun.

The matrix is shown in the Hall of God. Serapha is to be aware of yourself and to employ the analyzing male part of your mind to think about your place in the grand scheme of creation. Cheruba means your ability to listen to the intuitive voice of the emotional female part of your mind, and feel what is right or wrong for you. Lucifera is the truth as you see it freely spoken, including your ability to actively listen to others, and including your ability to admit mistakes. God symbolizes the higher cause you engage yourself in when living on planet Earth. The highest cause always is: Go there yourself and see the Light, which means: Find the answer to the questions, *Who are you? What is your place the society you live in? And what is your place in the grand scheme of creation?* Find the answer yourself, let nobody else answer the question for you. You walk along your path to God or to Enlightenment, or whatever you choose to call it, and pick up every little bit of wisdom and knowledge you can find. Then you will choose for yourself whether it is true for you or not. If it is not true for you, drop it with respect and keep what you need. Since all wisdom and all knowledge is part of the All-Including Truth, they all lead you in the same direction.

The Diamond and the matrix are implanted parts of every human soul and not to erase. How far the matrix is activated that it can do it's work depends on the depth and the persistence of your questioning yourself in search of the Philosopher's Stone.

The next plane is your mental universe, or your mind. It shows the Scroll of Memories that runs back to your very beginning. You write into the scroll every second of your present time, and you note how you value each incident on you own individual Scale of Values as it is valid at the time of the incident. Nothing that once is engraved on the scroll can ever be erased, but you are free to re-evaluate and attach new values to every incident of your life in the past.

Another part of your mind is the Book of Rules you live by. You are the only one who is entitled to write in your Book of Rules, and you are entitled to re-write your rules as much as you want to, provided nobody else is hurt by it. But as long as a rule is valid, stick to it. Changing rules in mid-game is rightly considered as unfair and foul game. One goal of the game is to find a set of rules you can stick to with greatest joy for the rest of your life without creating difficulties for yourself and your co-players.

The square surrounded by a circle is the male power inside the female power in your emotional body. The female part is the receptor of beauty and harmonies, and the source of gratitude, the male part is the source of inspired art.

Below your mental universe lies the plane of your material body and all the material things you are responsible for. The green aura surrounding the body symbolizes the Energy of Life that keeps your body ticking until it dies.

The spheres in the hands of the dancer show that you are but one link of the never-ending chain of taking and giving, of procreating and dying.

The skull shows that your material body one day will end existing, just like the whole material universe, shown by the stars, the clouds, and the spiral the dancer stands in. With the death of your material body, your emotional body and your book of knowledge and rules will die, too, but the scroll of your memories will never die. You, the eternal individual soul, will continue to be a self-aware part of the Absolute Truth.

As long as YouSoul live in your material body you are bound to the material world with it's laws of physics and biology and with it's built-in dualism. It is self-destructive to strive for release from the material world to become free before your body actually dies. Equally self-destructive is the longing for the unification of yin and yang to overcome dualism, because we live of the tension between the two. You are a full woman and not half a woman plus half a man—and Thanx to the Goddess for it. So enjoy your life on the surface of planet Earth. Enjoy, dance, make your life a celebration of life, love, and beauty and share your joy of life with everyone you meet, including cockroaches and chicken.

Source: Part of my papers I had to do for my exam to become a "responsible adult male human being," and I assure you that I had to do it over and over again, till Lilith was satisfied with my understanding, because she claimed: "I don't care how *good* you draw. I care about *what* you draw, because what you are able to draw, you understand."

65 — Your Leading Angel

Your angels are that part of you that is self-aware.
Your Higher Self.
Your spiritual leaders, or masters, or teachers.
Can also be your power animals, or crystals, or flowers, in fact, everything that keeps you grounded in the spiritual universe reminding you that there is more than money and success as defined by the leaders of human societies.

But all these are pretty imprecise expressions. Your Leading Angel is what you remember about yourself, if maybe only in parts: That your are a perfect hologram of the SupremeBeing, and she also knows what you are striving for, even if you don't remember it yet.

But it is easier and more beautiful, and within the laws of dualism it makes sense, to perceive your angels as separate but identical twin beings and connect with them, as long as you don't forget that your Leading Angel is your memory of yourself as a perfect spiritual being, which is what you really are. You need to know: You did not forget that you are a perfect spiritual being because you are stupid, or have

bad Karma, but this forgetting is part of the game of life because a game is not possible when you know everything beforehand. It is also a part of the game of life to strive for perfection by daily learning and improving yourself to enable yourself to play better games.

Your Leading Angel tells you constantly about the Hall of God and the Total Truth and how she would react in your situation, but she can't force you to act as she suggests. Sometimes you can hear her voice clearly, sometimes you can't hear her at all because you're busy with your own little games and problems, but that doesn't mean that she is silent.

Through your angels you are anchored in the spiritual universe, but there is one problem: You can imagine the Hall of God and the Host of Heaven, but you can't see them with your Earth-eyes, and your angels can imagine the material universe where you live right now, but they can't see it, because they have no Earth-eyes. They don't even know how your material body looks like, they have no idea how you feel about your body and how you feel about your actions within nature and within human society on planet Earth.

The card shows you as a dancer through human life in the small figure. Your Leading Angel is the big figure with Lucifera's golden mask. The blue arc above you is Vala's Veil of Illusions. It is placed between you and the spiritual universe which is shown as the Diamond of the All-Including Truth within the rainbow of the spiritual universe. The veil means that you have forgotten and don't yet remember who you really are.

Source: Unknown.

66 — Your Guardian Angel

The Angel of Your Past.

Your conscience (*Gewissen* in German).

She is the mirror that reflects your thoughts, words, your actions and your feelings about them. She is always a little later than you, like a mirror has first to see an image before it can reflect it. She is also the guardian of your self-awareness; she grows and becomes stronger with your growing self-awareness.

Your Guardian Angel shows you whether you acted right or wrong in any given situation, measured on your own perfection. Nota bene: Measured on *your own* perfection! Not measured on laws given by a god, or a pope, or an emperor, or whoever else. Only your own perfection is the yardstick. You alone are the maker of your laws, you alone are your judge using the mirror of your own perfection to validate your act, you alone dole out punishment or reward, which is either feeling bad or being pleased with yourself.

Just imagine yourself being a stiff-necked, stiff-eared donkey and your Leading Angel pulling in front and your Guardian Angel pushing

behind always in direction of perfection, and the Host of Heaven bursting with laughter because it is a very funny picture, indeed. Here fits the old proverb from the Canary Islands: You can force the donkey to the well but you can't force it to drink.

Mistake me not, that stiff neck and the stiff ears are your honor and your pride as a human being. You have the right, even the duty, to exercise your free will, because spiritual beings in human bodies are the only beings in the whole spiritual universe that own free will and free decision—even your angels are mirror-bound to you. You decide for them, but they can't decide for you. Without the quirks of human free decision the spiritual universe would be a deadly boring place and Earth would be like a stage without a show, and the Hosts of Heaven know it and because we entertain them with our quirks, they love us so dearly.

Here again you are shown in your material body and with you is your Guardian Angel with Lucifera's golden mask carrying the flame ball of the true teachings. Above Vala's Veil of Illusions soars Serapha, the Defense of the Honor of God and Goddess, to help you to measure every of your actions on the honor of The Powers-GreaterThanYou. On both your angel cards you are shown dancing in a golden background without structure to show that your angels can't see the material universe; they don't know how your body looks, they have no idea where you are hanging out right now, or what you are busy with. But they know precisely how you feel about you body, about your present time situation, and about your present time actions, and they know everything you learned by experience and how you feel about it.

LilithYggdrasil / Lectures
About Old And Young Souls

We teach that there is no such thing as old or young souls, because a soul—being a part of the spiritual universe—is as timeless as the spiritual universe itself.

Reasoning:

All religions on planet Earth teach independently in one form or the other that a soul is a member and a part of the spiritual universe, and that a soul is the creation of the SupremeBeing in it's image.

All religions without exception also postulate that the material universe, including the human body, is a creation of a PowerGreaterThanUs, and thus secondary to the spiritual universe.

The science of physics teaches that time exists only in the universe of SpaceMatterEnergy because "time comes into existence when matter driven by energy moves through space," which backtracking logically implies that a soul—being without SpaceMatterEnergy—is timeless.

That means for Our teachings: The concept of "soul" in connection with the concept of "old" or "young" is a contradiction in itself because old/young is the comparison of two different beginnings on the same time Line in the same space.

The words "old soul" or "young soul" probably express the idea that some of our fellow humans started the chain of incarnations on planet Earth earlier, which means that their memories reach further back into the history of human kind, which makes them appear older.

Or, a soul in a human body who busies herself more with the spiritual and mental worlds than with the material world appears to be older in the sense of being wiser.

So We think it better use of language not to say old or young soul but to say "early or late incarnation into a human body on planet Earth," or "someone who remembers more about former lives," or "a spiritually advanced, or more evolved, human."

The logical end of this chain of thought is: The soul is eternal—without beginning, with no end, which is one characteristic of the SupremeBeing, and the soul is timeless, which another characteristic of the SupremeBeing.

Therefore We teach: The soul is a hologram of the SupremeBeing—each soul is part of the SupremeBeing.

All souls together are the SupremeBeing like the individual grains of sand that form an endless beach.

Yours truly, LilithYggdrasil
HighPriestess in Service of AboraMana

67 — The Book of Rules

Never give what you do not want for yourself. This card helps you to recall the rules you voluntarily accepted as binding before you decided to come back to Earth to live a whole life long in a human body. They are carved in stone, you can't change them and they are not negotiable. They are valid for all humans in the past and present and they will be valid as long as a material universe and humans exist. You can't even contravene those rules, therefore it is better to know them well, that you can take advantage of them for your own benefit and those of your fellow human beings.

The Compass (up right): No matter in which direction you travel, the needle of the compass always shows the shortest way to the Light. Whether you pay attention and follow the needle or not is your free decision. Free means no fear of punishment, no hope of reward, only the consequences of your doings. You are a human being and not a dog in training.

The scale (upper left) has a golden and a black bowl as symbols for good or evil. The *Book of Rules* says: No matter what you do—

even when you do nothing—you throw a weight into one of the bowls of the scale.

The scale and the compass together are the symbol for your conscience, that what you are aware of being right or wrong. It has nothing to do with what somebody else told you of right and wrong. They symbolize your inborn ability to see, understand, and define the difference of good and evil, right and wrong. With the scale, your conscience measures the values of what you actually have done on the material plane.

Time and Death (far left): You are walking in an eternal present time against the unstoppable stream of time, which comes towards you from the future, and at the very end of your individual future on planet Earth stands your death. The Book of Rules says:

Your time is limited, but you don't know when your time ends.
There is no goal to reach, except the goals you set for yourself.
Except yourself, there is no one entitled to judge your performance.
There is no reward or punishment for your decisions and actions.
Every action or non-action has consequences.

The Spiral of Life (above center): The Book of Rules says: Move! No matter what you do, you move, either this way or that. This rule is reinforced by the above mentioned scale. No matter what you do, you throw a pebble in one of the bowls, and by doing that, you move on the spiral. It doesn't matter where on the spiral you stand at the moment; what matters is only the direction you move, or in which bowl you throw the pebble of your present moment's action. When you move to the inside, or throw your pebble in the black bowl, you become smaller until you drop into the Black Hole of Time. This is not a punishment; it is the natural consequence of your move in that direction.

When you move outside, you grow bigger and keep growing endlessly, and the more clear you will see the Light. This is not a reward, it is the natural consequence of your move in that direction. The compass and the scale let you know the direction you are heading. In the hollow of the spiral you find ten red fields. From the inside out they symbolize the most important emotional levels of a human: Apathy, sorrow, anger, hidden animosity, open rage, boredom, interest, enthusiasm, action. (Thanks to L. R. Hubbard.)

Decisions (below center): Making a decision (you can also call it making up your mind) is an analytical process influenced by your past experiences and your emotions about them, and biased by your hopes and fears. Making a decision includes the ability to see the consequences of that decision as far as possible in the future, as shown in the black and white squares. (Consequences are the results of your actions.)

The Book of Rules says: When you go *here* you can't go *there*. Which means that the whole future of the I-don't-go-*there* decision has disappeared in the Black Hole of Time. And it also means that you have to carry every consequence of your I-go-*here*-decision, whether you have foreseen them or not, whether you like them or not.

The game of chess and the game of pool teach you to see consequences. They also teach you the male virtue of placing your piece to your own advantage (which is cool) and to the disadvantage of your opponent (ask her about it).

68 — The Emotional Body

Praise, motivated by gratitude.
Awareness of beauty and harmonies in nature and art.
The source of the joy of life.
Wanting to share because of gratitude.

On the top of the card stands the Diamond of Total Truth surrounded by the spiritual universe. At the bottom lies the world of space, energy, matter, and time. Both are separated by the blue veil of illusions. Time is shown by the red squares and the clock at the bottom of the card. Some of the squares are broken to show the times when you are in stress and under pressure. The clock of gold and diamonds shows that you can't compensate your slavery to time by giving an irrational amount of energy for the symbol of your slavery.

Out of the chaotic matter with the red flames of anger, fight, and unhappiness grows a simple flower, to remind you that the beauty of AboraMana's children can be found in the very simple things of nature. Behind the flower is a fence. Fences and walls are the symbol

for fear—fear that something will enter the space you fenced in, or fear that something will break out that you want to keep in.

To rise above the level of the chaotic matter you might find yourself in, you have to employ the self-discipline of the male part of your emotional body, shown by the circle with the black rim, and give praise. To start the process you might have to ritualize your daily Prayer of Praise and Thanx until it continues on its own energy. Praise the flower, praise the child, your man, the cloud, or whatever you find, and do not forget to praise yourself and your own creations.

While doing that you'll find that the thing you praise will fill you with gratitude, which feeds the female part of your emotional body, shown by the circle with the white rim, which in turn naturally praises what fills her with gratitude. Praise is a natural expression of the joy of life and the greatest joy of life is gratitude for being alive and being able to enjoy the beauty of God's and AboraMana's creation.

The longer you do that, the closer together the male and the female parts of your emotional body move until they intersect. You become whole. Out of the intersection rises love, the circle with the red rim. Love will enable you to see through the Veil and catch a glimpse of the Total Truth. The higher above the material level your understanding, your gratitude and your love rise, the thinner the Veil becomes and the clearer and more complex your perception of the Total Truth becomes.

Source: Visualization of a conversation in a coffee shop in Kapa'a, Kaua'i.

69 — Communication

The mental body, the analyzing mind.
Logical chains of thought exchanged to either solve a problem or to inform each other about private windows.
The problem-oriented communication, where nobody attacks the other on the personal level, and everybody controls her ego so far that it doesn't interfere with the solving of the problem.
It also means to understand the difference between God's, AboraMana's, and human creation, and within the universe of human creation, it means to understand the difference between the creations of art and all other creations
Communication is only possible between persons who consider each other as equal.
Cutting communication is the last resort of someone who *must* be right, no matter how wrong she is.
Here we have a round table with a problem laying on top of it. Four persons—the golden globes—are gathered around it intending to solve that problem. The table is round to show that there is no

chairperson, no teacher, no leader, no one with the open or hidden intent to dominate the scene.

The symbols of the four Elemental Houses in the corners of the card suggest that the four persons are four distinct different individuals, with their different gender, backgrounds, and believes, but equal in their intent to solve the problem.

The green circle with the red square symbolize the women, the red square with the green circle symbolize the men. Those two different images also symbolize the emotional bodies of women and men. The emotional bodies of the four persons are connected with each other but they have no influence on the solving of the problem. That is why they are not connected to the golden globes.

The big heptagon is the Diamond of Total Truth. The splinters on the table need to be formed into the small heptagon of that part of the Total Truth all four persons can agree upon.

Source: Mosaic on a round table in the Hall of Justice in AtlantaCaldera. Ca 90 cm / 3 feet diameter. Contemporary, artist unknown.

70 – The LongHouse

Pictogram for House or Government. It shows a house on stilts, because the people who invented the pictogram live close to the ocean with heavy tidal waves. The house is divided into two equal parts by the main beam that carries the roof with the symbol of the black moon. The left side of the house belongs to the men, as indicated by Mars above their part of the roof; the right side belongs to the women, their star is Venus. The circle under the house is the fire where people gather around to talk about communal matters, again clearly divided into female and male matters.

The pictogram today is part of the Great Seal of AtlantaCaldera and symbolizes "We! The People."

Communal Affairs

It is *not* a sign of mental health to be well adjusted to a profoundly sick society.

Source: Written on a blackboard without credits.

Generally speaking, the male solution of communal affairs can be defined as:

Fear and distrust as underlying emotions and motivation of all thinking and acting.

Constant fight for dominance in a group.

Force, pressure, and social constraints as means of controlling the members of the group exercised by the alpha-males of the group and their accomplices.

Exaggerated honors for the alpha-males and their symbols—coats of arms, flags, national anthems, government palaces, parades, red carpets, and such like.

Narrow-minded national and territorial thinking with the symbols of fences and walls, borders and barriers, passports, visa, permits, and such.

War as accepted, often provoked, possibility to solve a problem, either a war of conquering to enlarge the own territory; or a war of suppression to force the loser to obey the winner, again because of economic or political reasons.

Winner-loser thinking with the symbols of prices, decorations, medals, titles.

Amassing private property and defending it by all means; exaggerated honors for the rich and famous, contempt for the poor. The generally accepted method of becoming rich is either outright robbery within all legality; or under-paying your workers and over-charging your customers.

Hardly any public property as compared to the amount of private property.

The public property is sadly neglected while the custodians of the property live in mansions.

Work motivated by money and/or prestige.

Relentless competition with a tremendous waste of resources to dominate, if possible wipe out, the competitors.

A very static social pyramid with a few extremely rich on top and masses of poor at the bottom.

Hostile to sex but a wild exaggeration of the importance of sports.

Revenge and punishment, including torture of body and mind, including ritual murder in form of death penalty.

This card asks: What do you do for the society you live in? For your group of friends? What do you give to the people you know and who support you, who are not your family?

The Little Black Book of the Tribune

honor the creations of nature
treat everything as if it is your own

keep your world clean
turn the wilderness of Earth into a garden
make the animals your friends
honor yourself
honor your ancestors
honor your parents
honor your marriage
honor your children
honor your tribe, your people, and your culture
honor the family, the tribe, the people, and the culture of others

give every human the same rights and possibilities
to live as you want and take for yourself
give only what you want for yourself
don't give something you don't want for yourself

don't envy a human because of her talents, position, or property

reduce your necessities
waste nothing, share your abundance
don't use your wealth to gather more wealth
don't abuse the trust somebody gave you
don't lie, cheat, or seduce

don't steal
don't destroy the property of someone else
be compassionate to everyone who is weaker than you
don't talk bad about someone else

don't kill the body of another human
don't injure the body of another human
don't torture the mind of another human
don't talk snotty to another human and don't cuss him

You / Second Set

Know Thyself

Who Are You? Define Yourself!

Also called Decisions

This is the area of your awareness and knowledge of yourself as an individual. It is presented to you in the male black/white, yes/no system instead of the female soft black/gray/white scale, because this way the questions are easier to understand and to answer. The two cards of each pair complement each other, that means: One helps you to understand the other.

Not always the card asks you a question. Sometimes, when the card or the explanation touches something inside you—when you understand the card well without knowing why, then it is your card. And then you should ask yourself: What does this card reflect in me?

The cards 02 – Serapha and 03 Cheruba belong not only to The Hall of God but also into this set, asking: Is your attention more on looking or more on listening? Do you love silence and the songs of nature more than music created by humans? Is it easier for you to gather information by words or by symbols or pictures?

You can also use the Devi and Deva (cards 30 to 37) of the Fifth Plane, Magic Biology, to help you define the sexual part of you. Then they can show you possible alternatives of the games you usually play in that area. That's why here follows a short definition of those cards:

30 – Devi of Orchid
Frankness in all erotic and sexual matters

31 – Deva of Colibri
Daydream, create art about sex and erotic

32 – Devi of Papaya
Being passive, letting your body being used

33 – Deva of Rooster
Disciplined Tantra practice

34 – Devi of Coral
Being aggressive, taking what you want

35 – Deva of Cowry
Active submission, the courtesan

36 – Devi of Oak
Active control of your man

37 – Deva of Lizard
Voluntary celibacy

The complete set of the decision cards (one pair of the Hall of God, four pairs of Devi and Deva, four pairs of Decisions) can give you a simplified picture of yourself if you did choose as honest with yourself as you were able.

You could also give this set to your potential mate and observe carefully how he defines himself, which makes it easier to decide whether you are compatible or not, because you will learn a lot about him.

There are many more of these kinds of questions. The ones presented here serve only to trigger finding and asking those questions yourself during the process of learning to know yourself.

Source: In a hidden part of our Central Library I found a book with over a thousand of those questions, collected by a scholar in ancient times. In his Foreword he wrote that he collected the questions for the fun of it, but the book should be kept secret because "finding the questions yourself is part of becoming self-aware; finding your own questions forces you to reflect about yourself and about your connections to the outside world."

So, for the sake of the game: Decide, knowing that the decision is valid only for now. And go and find your own questions about yourself.

First Pair 01
71 – The Naked Truth

*Believe nobody, question everything.
Go there yourself and look and experience.
Decide according to your own experiences.
Think and speak and act
according to your decisions.*

This card represents the Zen principle of clarity, simplicity, honesty in material, tools, and methods. No fringe, no frills. Decor very sparingly and only where it makes sense and never for it's own sake, not even for sentimental or nostalgic reasons.

Perfectionism.

It also means: Are you honest to yourself?

The prophet, the seer, the visionary.

A word of truth you can't understand without explanation of somebody else's is not *your* word of truth.

The courage to face the truth even if it hurts.

"Our Mother Goda Eva" is the title of the mythological First Woman. Goda means Daughter of the Goddess in the dialect of the farmers of AtlantaIsland. Eva (ancient Hebrew Havva) means Woman or Mother, extended meaning also The Beautiful.

She rises out of the male triangle like a green house filled with minerals, liquids, gases, and, to make it interacting, light and heat. This shows planet Earth as a closed system of physics with limited resources, without inflow from somewhere outside or drain to somewhere outside, as the sub-strata in which roots the entire biological life on the planet, including your and my biological body.

Eva is surrounded by the green aura of the Energy of Life which is shown by the green AboraMana as the Horned Goddess, who shines green through the blue body of Eva on those places where she is woman—her genital split, her womb, and her breasts.

Behind the Horned Goddess lies the male triangle as symbol of the creator of physics, which resonates with the lower triangle, and behind that stands the Diamond of Total Truth surrounded by the empty space of fantasy and imagination.

The Goddess—through Eva—holds the Mirror of Self-knowledge and the Apple of Awareness of Good and Evil.

The cloak around AboraMana's shoulder is the rainbow of the spiritual universe God dedicated to his MostBeloved "with Thanx for the songs your children dedicated to me," as the legend tells. Goda Eva is also permitted to wear the rainbow because she is the secondary creator of life, and because she was the first one to rise out of the animal consciousness to the self-awareness of a true human, and because she pulled her son, Adam, with her into the Light.

Source: The card shows a stained glass window in the fortress-church in the main village on the north eastern tip of AtlantaIsland, in the flatlands or lower farmlands as we call this area. Each square of the background is about one square foot. It was dedicated to the church by a man called Carlos, (or Carlito because he is so big and massive,) the owner of the "Fisherman's Sinkhole," a cave under the LighthouseRock in AtlantaCaldera he runs as a bar catering mostly to Barbar sailors.

First Pair 01
72 — The Veil of Maya

The half hidden, the charming
The package, not the contents.
The make-believe, the little charming lies, especially in cosmetics and fashion.
Social skills, which is not speaking and acting as you think and feel, but how it is political and socially correct. These abilities are important in every human society, but they have their time and place. Never to speak what you think and feel is either a sign of a liar who wants to take advantage of someone else or of a coward who is afraid of reprisals.
Shame disguised as modesty especially in the area of erotic and sex.
Self-deception, living by the lies about yourself. (*Lebenslüge* in German.)
Vanity, the bloated ego.
Fashion, face- and breast-lifting and that kind of surgery.
Living by the rules of others.
Being a victim of the opinions someone else might have about you.

Source: Costume and mask design for the carnival in honor of AboraMana depicting Vanity.

Second Pair 02
73 — Feathers

You have to swim against the stream if you want to drink clear water.
Be who you are and become who you can be.
Not all who wander are lost. Some drift, some search, but all are on a one-way-ticket.
Leave your sheltered home, open yourself for new experiences.
Active learning and actions for the benefit of the Higher Self (Soul), never being satisfied on the mental and spiritual level and the own abilities, constant self-improvement.
Careless about appearances, but perfectionist in all things concerning the self and the Burden (see below).
Living in the present on a day-to-day basis with a minimum of material possessions.
Wanderers resonate with the Elemental Houses of Air and Water; their sign is the mobile hanging on the upper left side of the card. It shows the apparent changeability and fickleness of wanderers swinging around a clearly defined Self (if only in parts) and a very stable inside-world.
The sliding doors to the left and the right open to the last stepping stones of what you are sure of, and the wide open water of uncertainties you'll have to cross. You don't know how this can be possible before you haven't left your last stepping stone irrevocable behind. But be assured that you will find a bridge, or a ford, or a boat to carry you across. Than you have to work you way through the jungle of a thousand possibilities and the fog of a thousand options. And the higher you climb the crystal mountain the clearer becomes

your Path, your goal, your spiritual universe, and your insight of the Total Truth.

On the left side in the shoulder bag you have the Burden you carry through your life, on the right side are your boots ready for you to step in and to go to places where you have never been before to find the best chances to grow mentally and spiritually. The burden symbolizes the specific Path through your life you have chosen to grow spiritually, mentally, and, if possible, materially till End of Game.

In the right frame of the door sticks a photo of your most beloved to remind you that you can't even take that when you go wandering because it ties part of your attention into the past instead of letting it free for the present and future.

It also says: No matter how I experienced my past, it brought me here to this point of my life, and because I'm happy right here and now, my past can't have been that bad because it was necessary.

The wandering life is a pilgrimage to a goal as you define it for yourself, shown by female-open shell of the old pilgrim's route to Santiago de Compostela in Northern Spain. The shell carries the sign of Venus, because you are a woman. Your lighthouse to the goal is Mars (at the very top), the symbol of your search is the red flower, both symbolizing male energy pulling you along your Path.

Wandering males carry a closed shell with the red sign of Mars. Their flower of search is blue, and their lighthouse to the goal is Venus.

The red flower is also the Holy Grail you potentially are. It will be filled with what you were searching for, which is to see the Total Truth, shown behind Mars.

Source: In memory of Tani San's House, Kyoto, Japan, winter 1972-1973.

Second Pair 02
74 — Roots

The gardener, the local.
Action for the benefit of the community.
Global thinking—local acting.
Long term planning, life in cycles.
Ecological consciousness.

Joy in the change of seasons and the weather. The ancient weather witches who were able to influence the weather through their exact knowledge of the meteorological conditions. The best example is the rain dance.

The wise one finds the whole world at her doorsteps.

The card shows a shamana ceremony during the planting of the first Taro root. She gathers Energy of Life from AboraMana's unlimited source, filters it through her body, and stores it in the mother plant. At the same time she releases her water into the mud hole she dug for the root to complete the cycle of taking and giving, and to ask GodFather to send rain.

Source: The *Book Of Legends For Children*. Inspired by the Taro fields of Hanalei, Kaua'i.

Third Pair 01
75 — TreeDweller

Daydreams.
Games played in your mind.
Daydreaming is one of the most precious abilities of a human being because it taps directly into the sphere of creativity that lies around the Diamond of Total Truth. It is an ability that can be learned or re-learned and should be trained carefully. Daydreams are the basics of all arts. Controlled daydreaming trains the ability to see a movie, to visualize a painting, to tell a story, to hear a song in your mind. It is the sphere where you are truly unlimited and free to dream up whatever you want, where you are closest to the powers of creativity, where you are in total control of everything that happens, where you are truly the Almighty Goddess of your spiritual and mental world.

The questions among others are: Do you think climbing trees is a worthwhile activity for a grown up? Do you like to stand high and look down? Do you like wind and wide open spaces?

Source: Sketch for a poster in the old style, showing the North shore of Kaua'i looking west to the NaPali (The Cliffs).

Third Pair 02
76 — CaveDweller

The introvert, the egocentric.
Withdrawn life, contemplation.
Also, fear to of strange people and new experiences.
Also, excessive use of alcohol and other legal or illegal drugs to numb yourself.
Escaping reality by watching TV, reading books.
Among others, the questions are: Do you like closed rooms, closed doors, curtains? Do you like to decorate your home?

Source: The cave I used as a studio on La Palma Island above the Puerto de Tazacorte. This is where the Goddess began channeling.

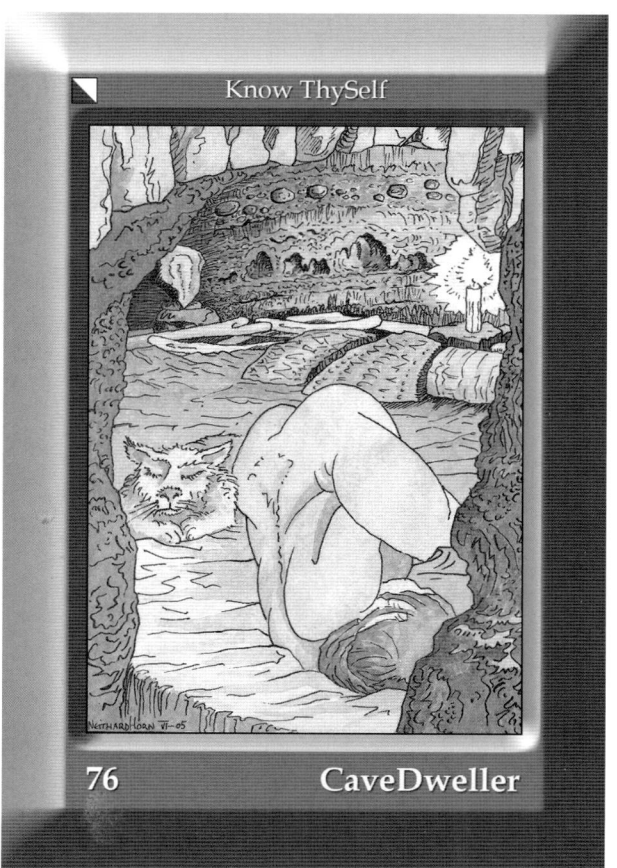

Fourth Pair 01

77 — Day

Day, sun, male, gold, fire.
She asks: Are you a day-person?
Independent thinking.
Clarity, honesty, industry.
City-life, the universe created by humans: Culture, civilization, technology.
Sola LilitWisdom: Waste nothing, share everything, plant Taro, praise the Goddess, and we all will live in abundance. (Taro stands for the human business to grow food for survival. You can eat Taro, but you can't eat money.)
The questions are: Do you go early to bed and rise early? Do you like electric light? Or natural light, sunlight or moonlight?

Source: A Prayer of Thanx to the Rising Sun, Kapa'a Beach, Kaua'i.

Fourth Pair 02
78 — Night

Night, moon, female, silver, water
Country life, nature, the universe created by God and Goddess.
Liberty of emotions, i.e., not stuck in one emotion but free floating as the present time situation demands.
Free of fears; free of inhibitions.
Compassion, ecstasy.
She asks: Are you a night-person? Do you like the darkness of night without electric light?
When I was digging in the dusty corners of our Central Library in search of old cards for the deck, I found a piece of vellum covered with our ancient script. Obviously it is a record of government-policy of an early LilithYggdrasil:

"Moona LilitPeace will reign when every woman can dance, naked if she wants to, in the darkest parks of our cities without risking to be molested by a man,

"when every girl can travel freely and without fear to the remotest corners of our planet, and everyone will help her along to the goal,

"when we do not need locks or walls anymore to protect our honest property because we have learned not to take what is not ours, and because we have learned to share.

"I know that this is possible, I know that humans are able to do it. They know the difference between good and evil, they have the sacred gift of free decision, they are the most beloved children of creation, there is no evil in them unless it is put there by another human."

Yours truly, LilithYggdrasil

In the same corner I found the following text, and I think Lilith put it there especially for me to find it and to pass it on to you:

The Secret Archives of LilithYggdrasil

Humans look into the future
waiting for the AntiChrist
but smart as he is he has hidden in the past,
and we all know his name.

Everything that is rotting human society
you can read in his teachings,
which are against Christ's teachings.

Christ is a HolySpiritMan—
AntiChrist makes him a Saving God.

Christ teaches a loving God,
teaches peace of mind and joy in God—
AntiChrist teaches a revenging God,
teaches fear, fire, and brimstone,
teaches to murder the body to save the Soul.

Christ loved and respected women—
AntiChrist teaches to suppress them.

Christ teaches to hold on to the law
and not to change it—
AntiChrist tells you no need to obey the law
as long as you believe
what he tells you about Christ.

There is no DevilSatan, there is no Hell.
There is no God who judges you,
rewards you or condemns you.
You need no Christ to save you,
because you are not lost.

End of Game

79 — Eternity

The circles of sun and moon, and the cycle of life and death define our concept of time and eternity. Infinity and Eternity are primary parts of the Absolute. That is why we can't really understand them. We consider infinity as analytical male understanding, connected to the universe of physics referring to distance and number; and the concept of eternity as emotional female understanding connected to the biological universe referring to time.

The card does not only show the Hall of God in clouds and rain and rainbow, the ocean, the sky and the sun (the universe of physics) as symbol for infinity, but also flowers, palm trees, and a broaching Humpback Whale (the universe of biology) as symbol for eternity, who carry the drive for endlessness not as individuals, but as part of the chain of life of the species.

You are part of eternity—not you as a material woman, who one day will die, but you as part of the chain that receives and passes on not only the spark of life for humankind but also the codes of human behavior and the history of humankind.

Large parts of what today we call civilization is the influence of women upon men. Women invented spinning, weaving, the dying of fabrics. They developed gardening, irrigation, and the conservation of food. They were patient and loving enough to tame animals and out of that they started selective breeding. They invented pottery and the first art as they decorated their pots with scratched and stamped patterns. They discovered music in the rhythm of pestle and mortar as they crushed barley and millet, and then they danced to the music. They invented literature as they told their children the first goodnight-stories. And this goes on and on, and it is not even safe to say who really invented the wheel and tamed the fire.

To show you only one example: In the times of the Troubadours, women dictated men's grooming, clothing, table manners, education, and skills in music, dancing, and poetry for truly the objective better of all involved, naturally only in the noble class, which like every class- and caste-system, an antisocial invention of men.

So please be careful about what you pass on into the future, into what for us is eternity, because you are not only responsible for the future of your children but also for your own future because always remember: Your own children one day might be your parents.

This card asks you to go out into the next park and observe how young mothers treat their children. Then ask yourself: Do I want to be treated like that by the mother of my next body? To know: Most mothers treat their children as they have been treated themselves by their mothers.

Source: The Hall of God as seen from planet Earth. Kapa'a Beach, looking south.

The Backside of the Cards

The backside shows the Diamond of the All-Including Truth and the flaming ball of the pure teachings to show that this deck of cards is a book of lessons that can help you to enlarge your private window that you can see a new facet of the Diamond by becoming aware of a new concept of thinking and perception.

The square, like a door to a vault, suggests that behind the door there is something precious hidden. It also corresponds with the high-tech appearance of the frames of the front side, and it suggests that this deck comes from another world, from a mirror-earth.

Laying Out and Reading the Cards

When reading the cards, remember they don't give answers to questions you might have. The cards question *you*, and you have to find your own answers; your layout is the Magic Mirror you can see yourself in; where you question not only yourself, but also everything you know and consider as true. To become more self-aware is what the game is about.

The Cosmic Net

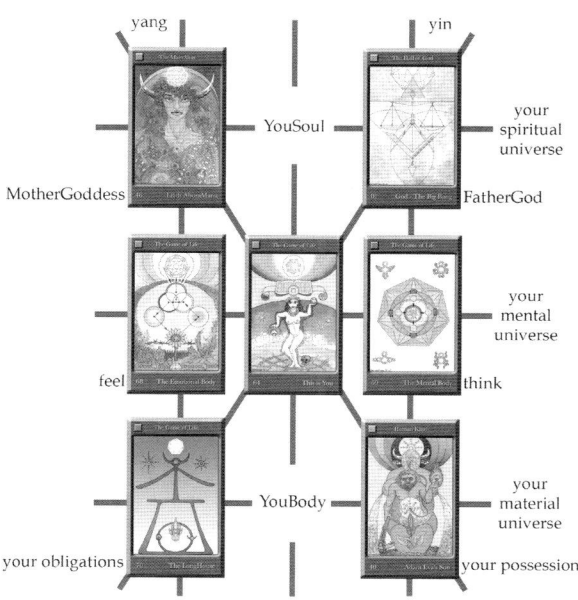

The Basic Layout Showing the *Why* of the Layout

The top row shows your spiritual universe. The left-hand side of the row is YANG, FEMININE, GODDESS; the right-hand side is YIN, MASCULINE, GOD.

The middle row is your mental universe. Yang is your feelings, yin is your analytical thinking. The card in the center is you, here, now, laying out the cards, wanting to know more about yourself.

This card (called the YOUCARD) you can push up and see yourself as a Soul, as a part of the spiritual universe, as a member of the Host of Heaven, as the child of your Divine Parents. When you push it down you see yourself as a material human body with all that this implies.

The bottom row shows your MATERIAL UNIVERSE. On the yang side are your connections to your social environment, including your family, and your obligations towards individual members of society, and towards your society in general; the yin side are your possessions, and every material thing you are responsible for.

Laying Out The Cards

First Step

Separate the ZeroCard and place it above all other cards. Whatever you play with the deck, the Zero-Card is set apart to remind you that whatever you read in the cards is part of the All-Including Truth.

Second Step

Take the Jokers out of the deck. Shuffle the two sets of the jokers separately and choose one card of each set.

First: Place your FateCard open next to the ZeroCard as shown in the illustration.

Fate is what is given to you and what you can't change; that's why it is on the passive or yang-side.

Second: Place the open WarriorGoddess beside your FateCard.

Your Fighting Spirit is the talents you have been given with the obligation to train and better them each day at least a little bit. That's why it is on the active or yin-side.

Third Step

Shuffle the remaining deck, spread them backside up flat on the table. Choose one card after another and lay them out, one after the other, backside up, in form of an H. The order of laying them out is your choice, lay them out in the order that feels best to you, but make sure you remember the order, for you open them in the same order.

Fourth Step

Open the first card in the order you laid it out, contemplate it, open the next card, contemplate it, and so on.

When you are done opening and contemplating each card solo, look at the whole picture, up and down on both sides, left to right on all three levels, and diagonally from the top corners to the bottom corners and back up again. See yourself as the central knot of your personal piece of the Cosmic Net.

Then see the loose ends of the strings of your personal Net as ending in a knot in the Net of your next human, or animal, or plant, or whatever parts of Creation you are connected with here, now, in present time.

Remember: You are one knot in the Cosmic Net and your strings reach further out than you might think—one of your strings reached out to me, although I don't you.

Aloha and Mahalo

Aloha, Welcome Home, and Mahalo, Thanks for Coming!

Yours truly,
Neithard Horn

PostScript

One moonless night at the beach of Kapa'a, homeless and hungry, I asked the Heavens above: "Why me?" and I heard Lilit's voice booming among the stars, humbling and mocking me:

"Because you're there, you fool. And because I trained you until I deemed you fit to do the job for me— and admit you enjoyed it."

Yes, I did.

My work is done, AboraMana's message is in your hands; my body is old and I wait every day to be called home. May the Goddess of Life have mercy that She takes back Her Energy without doing my body pain.

About the Author

Neithard Horn was born 07 October 1939 in the early morning, right in the middle of Nazi-Germany, just a few weeks after Hitler had started the Second World War. He is a Double Libra and belongs to the House of Air. In the deck of AboraMana the cards of his choice are: 71 – The Naked Truth, 73 – Feathers, 75 – TreeDweller, and 77 – Day.

He was raised in Germany under three different political systems, which made him later an anarchist, cosmopolitan, and peacenik. He is a first-generation hippie, a lopsided talented late-bloomer, a tree-frog-green idealistic dreamer, and more intelligent than is good for him, and therefore he's now living the life of a happy solitaire.

Instead of attending preschool, he found himself on the run before the Sowjet army, and in Germany being carpet-bombed, and he went to primary school in Sowjet-occupied Germany, learning Russian and the ideals of Stalin and his German cronies, being most of the time hungry and cold, running around in rags. He was fifteen years old when he jumped the fence to West-Germany, which at that time was still easy going. There he attended without any success secondary school, went through two years of agricultural training in the mountains of Bavaria, and attended, with slightly more success, agricultural college. And then, following a dream, he sailed in an immigration-Liner through Gibraltar, the Mediterranean, and the Suez Canal to Australia, where he worked as a cane cutter, cattle drover, fence builder, and well driller in North Central Queensland.

After two years, he sailed in a slow, old-fashioned freighter over the South Pacific islands, through the Panama Canal, the Caribic islands, over the Atlantic, through Gibraltar, back to Germany, where he was a student (the best of his class this time) and teacher of fine arts and crafts. After three years as a teacher, he dropped out because he didn't like the system he was working for and became instead a painting Zen monk in Japan, a good-for-nothing painting hippie in Vienna, a ship's carpenter and draftsman in Holland, and in the meantime he travelled Europe, Indonesia, and the Pacific Rim.

Since 1984, after the ship he was in went under in the English Channel, he has been a full-time visual artist and designer, a philosopher, and an independent student of metaphysics, human behavior, and ecology—besides art, naturally.

He lived from December 1999 to October 2004 in a cave on La Palma, Canary Islands, where the Goddess began channeling the images for the deck of cards AboraMana in your hands.

And now he lives on Kaua'i island.